ESSENTIAL NAPLAN

NUMERACY

NAPLAN*-Format Practice Tests with Worked Solutions

These tests have been produced by Five Senses Education Pty Ltd
ndependently of Australian governments and are not officially
endorsed publications of the NAPLAN program

EAR 4

RAY LEE | JIMMY LIU

To Cookie, my light,
and to Phoebe who I hope
can one day figure out all the questions in this book.

Five Senses Education Pty Ltd
2/195 Prospect Highway
Seven Hills 2147
New South Wales Australia

First Published 2023. Revised 2025.

Lee, Ray and Liu, Jimmy

Essential NAPLAN*
Numeracy Year 4
NAPLAN*-Format Practice Tests with Worked Solutions

ISBN 978-1-76032-550-3

2025 01 07

Contents

Preface

This book is designed to help students prepare for the NAPLAN Test. It consists of five numeracy practice exam papers and is suitable for use by Year 4 students. The exam papers are designed to the exact format of the NAPLAN Numeracy Test, with hand-picked questions that closely relate to past NAPLAN Examination questions.

Success in this competitive exam requires commitment and hard work. We hope these practice exam papers can help you achieve your goals.

Five Senses Education

Year 4 NAPLAN*-Format

NUMERACY PRACTICE TEST 1

Instructions

- There are 40 questions.
- You have 50 minutes to complete the test.
- You have to shade one bubble for each multiple-choice question.
- Write your answer in the box for short answer questions.

NAME : ______________________________ SCORE :____________

1 Which letter shows where the fraction $\frac{3}{5}$ should be placed on this number line?

2 Ian starts washing 10 cars at 10:30 am.

It takes him 15 minutes to wash each car.

What time will he finish washing the cars?

12:00 pm	12:30 pm	12:45 pm	1:00 pm
☐	☐	☐	☐

3 Lisa buys 6 oranges at 45c each.

She pays with a $20 note.

What change will she be given?

$16.90	$17.30	$17.90	$18.30
☐	☐	☐	☐

4 There were 1203 red buttons and 765 green buttons. Billy mixed them together and packed them equally in 8 boxes.

How many buttons were in each box?

246	264	1968	1978
☐	☐	☐	☐

5 The bar graph below shows the number of cars sold in a showroom from June to November.

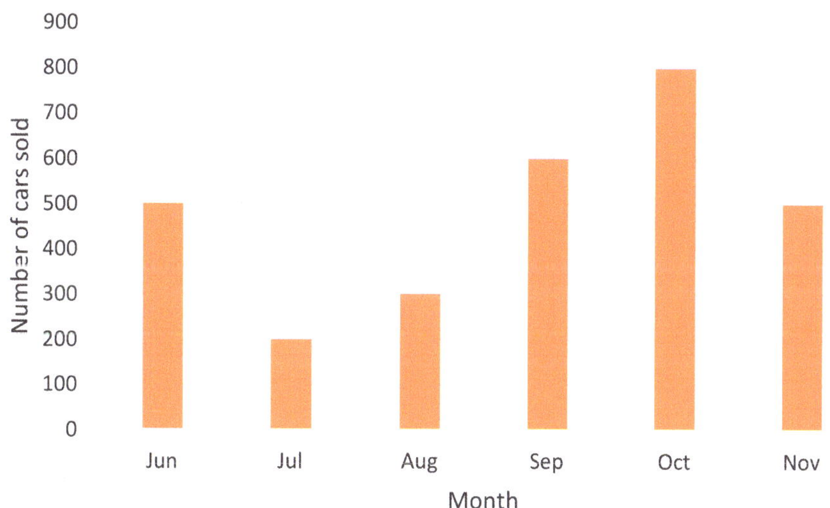

How many **more** cars were sold in October than in August?

☐

6 The table below shows a survey of 150 club members and the activities they participate in. Each club member is only allowed to participate in one activity.

Activities	Number of People
Folk Dancing	25
Playing Chess	58
Sailing	17
Cycling	45

How many people do **not** take part in activities at all?

5 ☐ 15 ☐ 20 ☐ 25 ☐

7 A table costs 6 times as much as a chair. If the chair costs $15, how much do the table and the chair cost altogether?

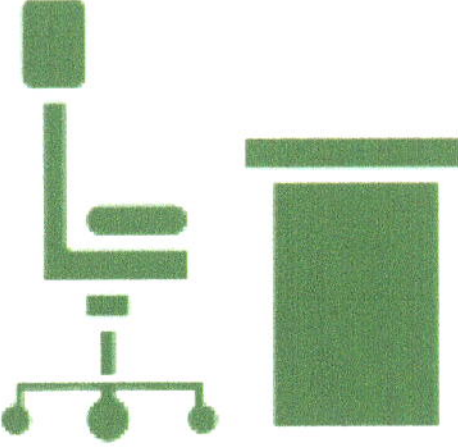

$21 ☐ $90 ☐ $96 ☐ $105 ☐

8 What is the next number in this pattern?

9 Which one of the following calculations has same value as 16 × 28 ?

- ☐ 16 × 20 + 8
- ☐ 16 × 8 + 20
- ☐ (16 × 20) + (16 × 8)
- ☐ 10 + 6 × 28

10 Michael signed up for art lessons during the school holidays. The clock showed the time he reached the art centre on the first day.
He was 45 minutes late. At what time, did the lesson start?

1:05 pm	1:45 pm	12:55 pm	12:45 pm
☐	☐	☐	☐

11 Mangoes cost \$8/kg and star fruit cost \$6/kg. If I bought $\frac{1}{4}$ kg of mangoes and $\frac{2}{3}$ kg of star fruit, how much did I pay?

\$8 per kg

\$6 per kg

☐

12 What is the least number of marbles I need if I need the amount to be equally spread amongst 2, 3, and 4 people?

- ☐ 6
- ☐ 8
- ☐ 12
- ☐ 21

13 There is $4\frac{1}{2}$ kg of sweet potato.

If Christina and her sister ate $1\frac{1}{3}$ kg together, how many kilograms are left?

☐

NUMERACY YEAR 4

14 In a long distance race around Sydney, Keith could only run one third of the way. If the race was 37.74 kilometres long, how far did Keith run?

12.38 km ☐   13.04 km ☐   12.73 km ☐   12.58 km ☐

15 When 200 people attended a concert, the concert hall was 80% full. What is the capacity of the hall?

200 ☐   250 ☐   300 ☐   350 ☐

16 If I went out to dinner with my 7 friends and everyone paid $13.50, how much did the meal cost?

☐

17 Choose the most economical purchase of rice.

- [ ] $50.00 per 10 kg bag
- [ ] $28.00 per 7 kg bag
- [ ] $17.00 per 5 kg bag
- [ ] $24.80 per 8 kg bag

18 Three squares of side 5 cm are placed together.

5 cm

What is the perimeter of this figure?

30 cm	40 cm	50 cm	60 cm
☐	☐	☐	☐

19 A box with 5 chocolates in it has a mass of 400 g.
The same box with 10 chocolates has a mass of 700 g.
What is the mass of one chocolate?

400 g

700 g

20 What is the area of the shaded part below?

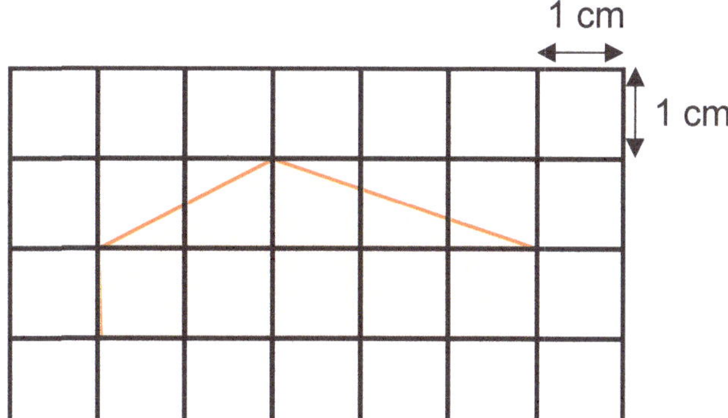

6.5 cm^2 ☐ 7 cm^2 ☐ 7.5 cm^2 ☐ 8 cm^2 ☐

21 The minute hand on this clock turns 300° clockwise.

What number is it now pointing to?

1 ☐ 3 ☐ 8 ☐ 10 ☐

22 Sam, Pam, Dan and Chan all together have $74.

If Sam has twice as much as Chan who has $3 more than Dan and $17 less than Pam, how much does Chan have?

$10 ☐ $12 ☐ $14 ☐ $16 ☐

23 Suzie has 21 marbles. After buying some more, she has three times her original amount. She then lost 8, and found 2. Her friend gave her 9 more.

How many does she have now?

48 ☐ 53 ☐ 66 ☐ 78 ☐

24 The ratio of the width of a rectangle to its length is 4:5.
If its length is 20 cm, what is the width of this shape?

20 cm

?

12 cm ☐ 15 cm ☐ 16 cm ☐ 24 cm ☐

25 I have a certain number. When I multiplied it by 4, subtracted 2, added 9, and divided this result by 3, I got 9.

What was my number?

☐ → × 4 → − 2 → + 9 → ÷ 3 → 9

26 A certain restaurant makes one pizza in 15 minutes.

How long will it take them to make 16 pizzas?

[ ] hours

27 Which of the following views is correct for the following composite shape?

Front view

Top view [ ]

Right side view [ ]

Left side view [ ]

Front view [ ]

28 What is the volume of a cube with side length 8 cm?

[ ]

8 cm

29 Stephen is making sandwiches using the breads, spreads and fillings shown in the table below.

Bread	Spread	Filling
White	Butter	Cheese
Brown	Mayonnaise	Egg

How many different types of sandwiches can he make?

3 ☐ 6 ☐ 8 ☐ 12 ☐

30 The pie graph below shows Year 4 students' favourite sports. Each student only picked one favourite sport.

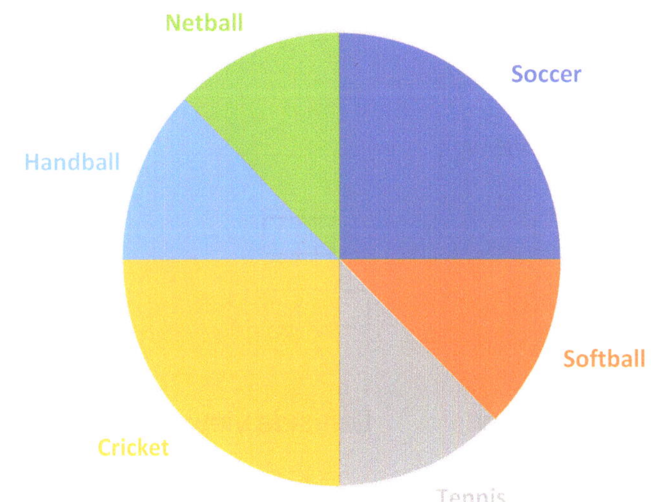

What percentage of students chose soccer or tennis?

12.5% ☐ 25% ☐ 37.5% ☐ 40% ☐

31 The table below shows the number of messages Paul sent using his mobile phone for the last three days.

Day	Thursday	Friday	Saturday
No. of messages	52	14	69

What was the average number of messages Paul sent each day?

36 ☐ 45 ☐ 47 ☐ 50 ☐

32 Vivian recorded the lowest temperatures over four days in winter.
Which temperature was the coldest?

	Monday	Tuesday	Wednesday	Thursday
Temperature	11.5°C	11.05°C	10.45°C	10.5°C

11.5°C ☐ 11.05°C ☐ 10.45°C ☐ 10.5°C ☐

33 Karen's hair grows about 13.5 centimetres per year.

Karen did not have a haircut for 4 years.

How much has her hair grown?

0.054 metre ☐ 5.4 metres ☐ 5.4 centimetres ☐ 54 centimetres ☐

34 You have two flat pieces of metal as shown to the right.
You are not allowed to bend them, or put one piece on top of the other.

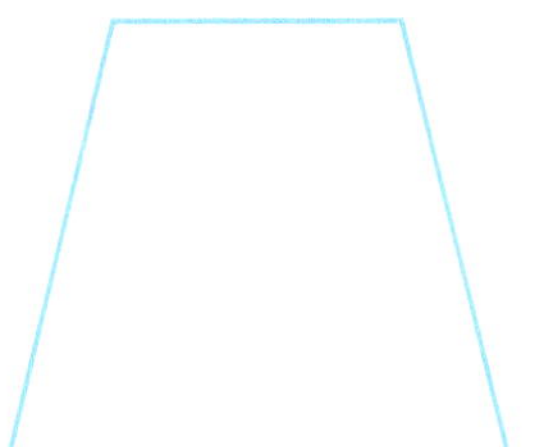

Which of the following shapes could you make?

A square ▭ A rectangle ▭ A rhombus ▭ A parallelogram ▭

35 Alan, Benny, Chris and Daniel each have a box of tiles.
The tiles are square and measure 1 cm by 1 cm.
Alan has 20 tiles, Benny has 22 tiles, Chris has 24 tiles and Daniel has 26 tiles.

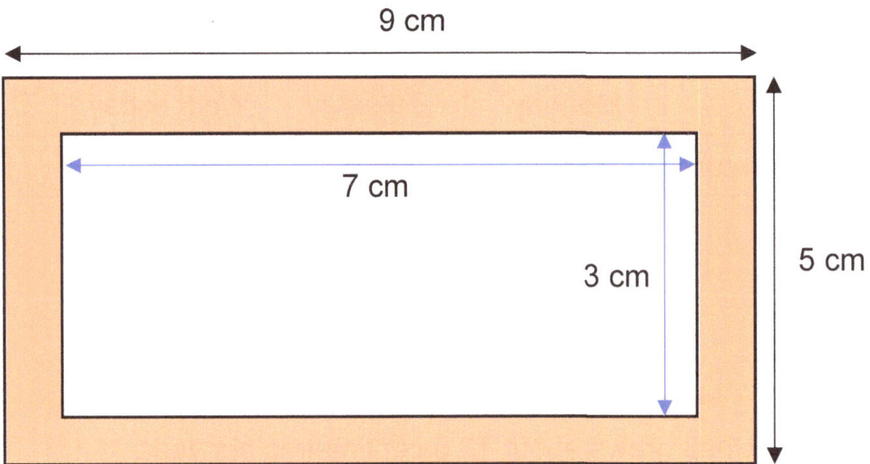

Who can use their tiles to exactly cover the shaded area?

Alan ▭ Benny ▭ Chris ▭ Daniel ▭

NUMERACY YEAR 4

36 Choose the shape that will join with the figure below without gaps.

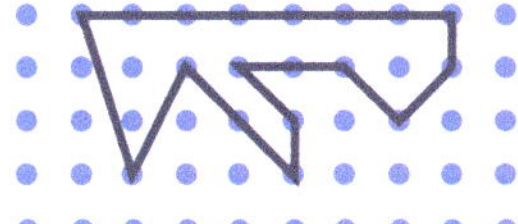

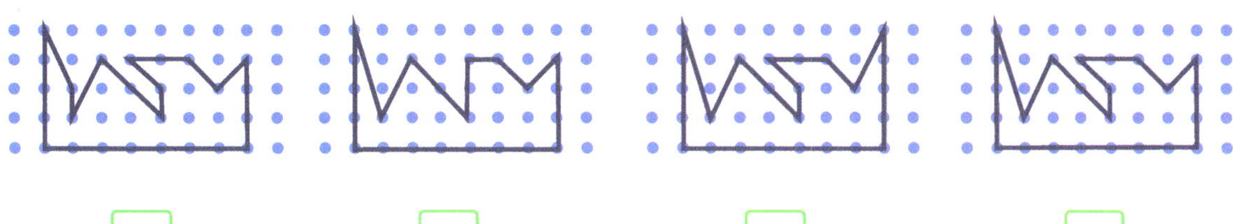

37 Which shape would I get if I put my pencil at point X and followed the given directions?

South 2 cm, East 3 cm, North West 5 cm, West 1 cm.

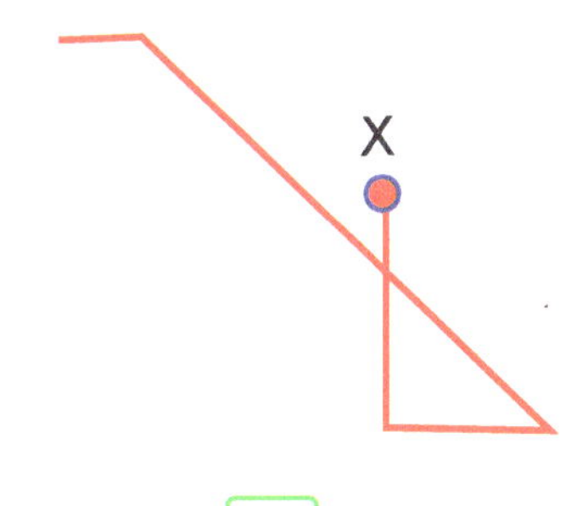

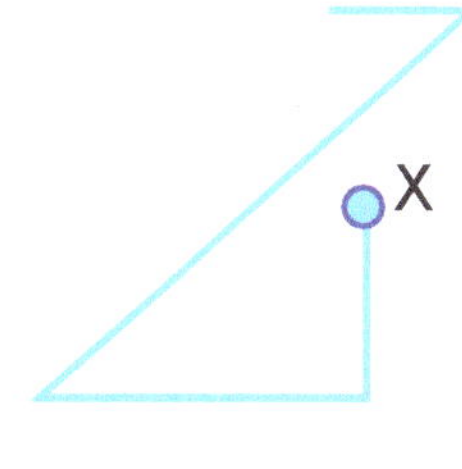

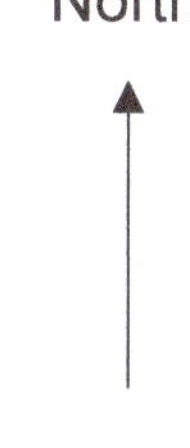

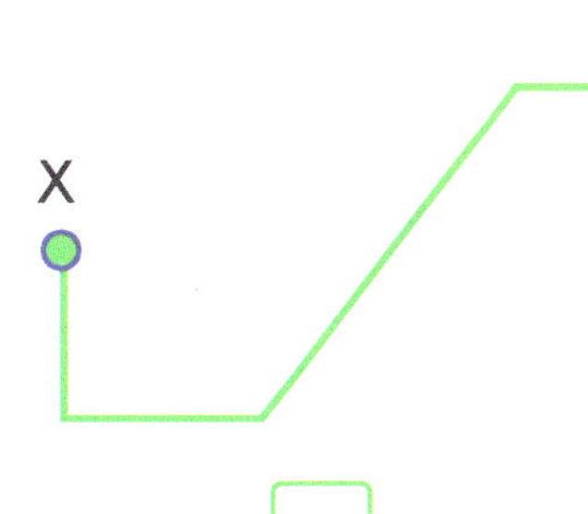

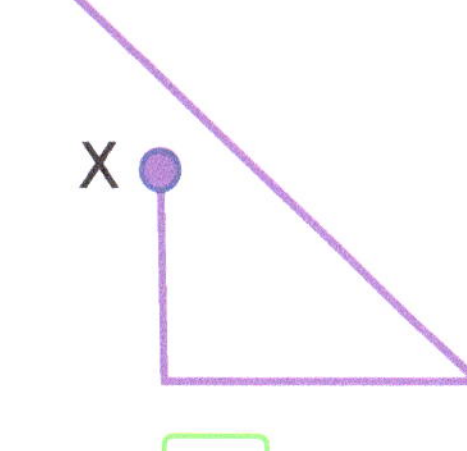

38 How much does a block of metal weigh if one quarter of it is 300 grams less than one half of it?

[ ] kg

39 What shapes will be left in circles A, B, and C if we take away all the shapes that are in B and C?

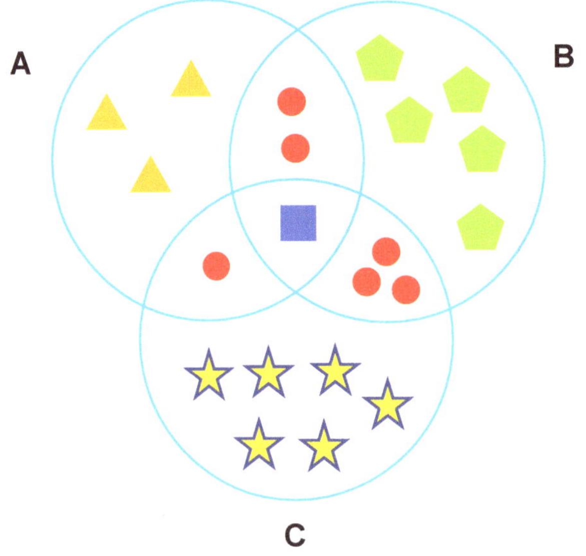

triangles ☐ a square ☐ circles ☐ stars ☐

40 Points W, X and Y lie on the corners of a rectangle as shown below.
Point Z lies on the fourth corner of the rectangle.
What are the coordinates of point Z?

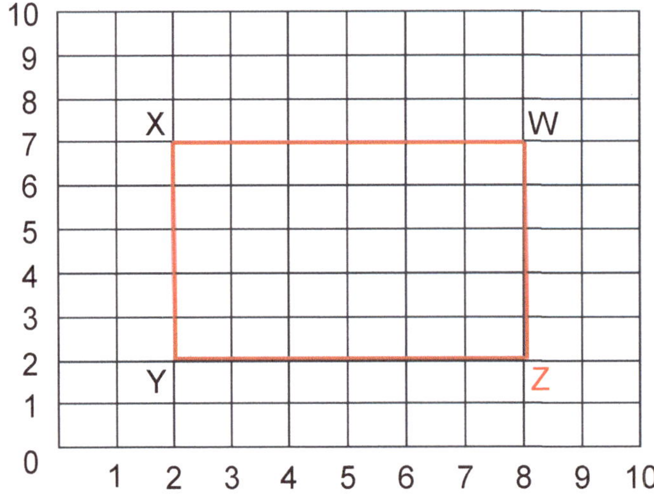

(2, 8) ☐ (8, 2) ☐ (7, 2) ☐ (7, 8) ☐

Year 4 NAPLAN*-Format

NUMERACY PRACTICE TEST 2

Instructions

- There are 40 questions.
- You have 50 minutes to complete the test.
- You have to shade one bubble for each multiple-choice question.
- Write your answer in the box for short answer questions.

NAME : ______________________ **SCORE :**__________

1 Olivia measures the length of a playground with a stick.

The playground is 35 stick lengths long.

The stick is 45 cm long.

How long is the playground?

1575 m ☐ 157.5 m ☐ 15.75 m ☐ 1.575 m ☐

2 Jessica buys a glass of juice and a cookie as per the prices below.

How much change does she get from $10.00?

$6.80 **$2.95**

☐

3 Rick is trying to make the largest number possible from the digits 1, 4, 8 and 9.

If the 9 must go in the ones column, what is the largest number Rick can make?

1 4 8 9

☐

NUMERACY YEAR 4

4 My bucket slowly leaks water. At the beginning of the day, there was 5000 mL, but I lost 1349 mL and another amount before the end of the day. I ended the day with 2000 mL. What was the second amount I lost?

1651 mL ☐ 1751 mL ☐ 1851 mL ☐ 1951 mL ☐

5 Below are a set of spelling test scores out of 10 marks for a group of 55 students.

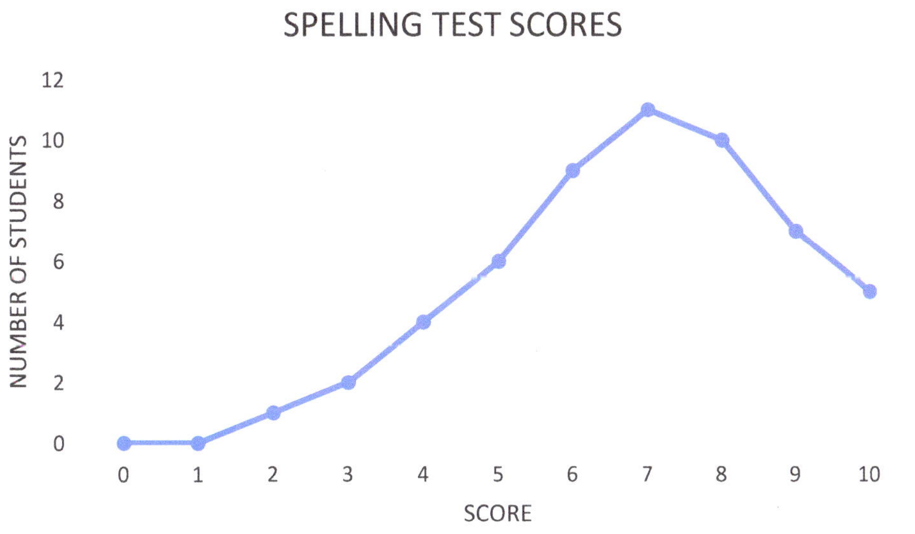

SPELLING TEST SCORES

NUMBER OF STUDENTS
12
10
8
6
4
2
0
0 1 2 3 4 5 6 7 8 9 10
SCORE

How many students scored more than 8?

5 ☐ 7 ☐ 10 ☐ 12 ☐

6 The usual price of a guitar is $300. At a sale it was reduced it by 20%.

What was the sale price?

20% off

$200 ☐ $220 ☐ $240 ☐ $260 ☐

7 The following graph compares how far 4 athletes ran with how much water they drank.

Water drank

Andrew Dennis

Jonathan Benny

Distance

Who was the most efficient athlete?

Andrew ☐ Dennis ☐ Jonathan ☐ Benny ☐

NUMERACY YEAR 4

8 Liam bought a motorcycle for which he paid a deposit of $320 and 12 monthly instalments of $25 each. Find the cost of the motorcycle.

9 Mrs Lin used $\frac{3}{8}$ of a bag of flour to bake cakes and $\frac{1}{5}$ of the remainder to bake biscuits. What fraction of the flour did she use altogether?

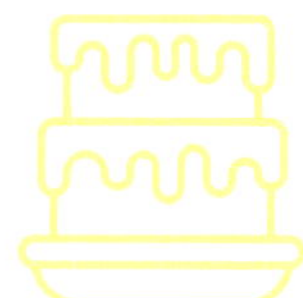

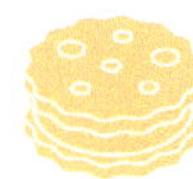

10 The ratio of the number of female members to the number of male members in a club is 2:3. If there are 10 female members, how many members are there altogether?

10 ☐ 15 ☐ 20 ☐ 25 ☐

11 Watermelon fruit costs \$7.95/kg. How much would 3 kg cost?

\$7.95/kg

12 Find the area of the shaded part of the rectangle.

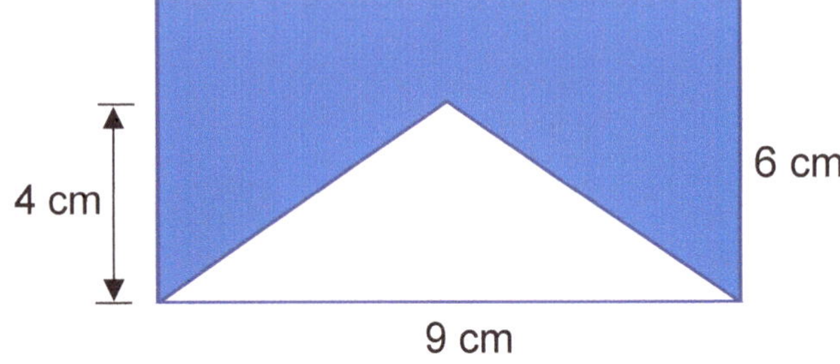

cm^2

13 The clock shows the time Mary arrived at school.

If she arrives home 7.5 hours later, what time will it be?

2:30 pm	3:00 pm	3:30 pm	4:30 pm
☐	☐	☐	☐

NUMERACY YEAR 4

14 Use the following clues to identify the solid.

It has seven faces. It has 12 edges. It has seven corners.

It is ☐

a cube ☐ a triangular prism ☐ a cylinder ☐ a hexagonal pyramid ☐

15 If these nets are folded to make dice and then rolled on the table, which one would be most likely to show a two?

	3	
	2	4
5	6	
	1	

	3	
	2	3
4	5	
	2	

	5	
	2	5
2	5	
	2	

	2	
	6	5
6	2	
	4	

☐ ☐ ☐ ☐

16 I need 27 cubes to make a 3 x 3 x 3 stack as shown below.

How many cubes do I need to make a 6 x 6 x 6 stack?

18 ☐ 54 ☐ 128 ☐ 216 ☐

17 Below is a group of shapes.

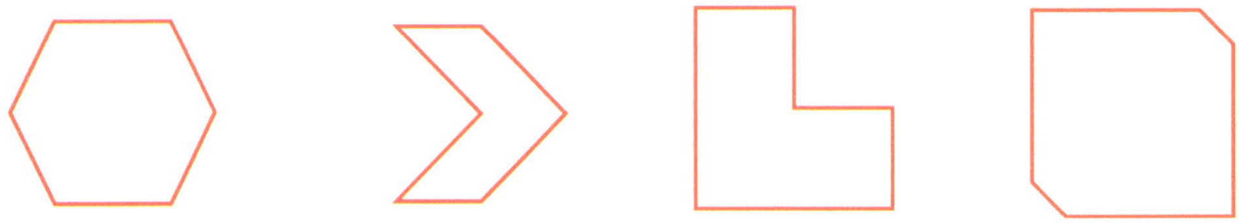

Which shape belongs in this group?

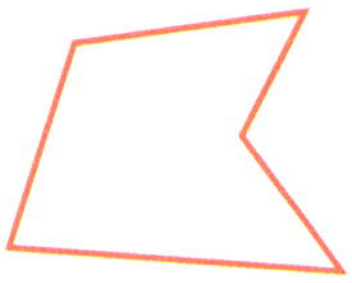

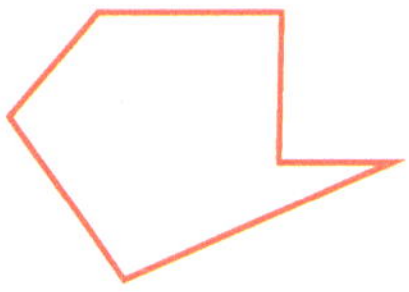

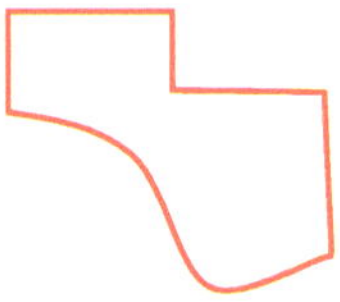

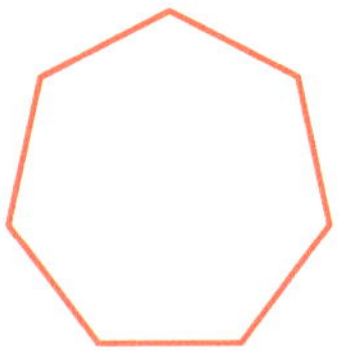

☐ ☐ ☐ ☐

18 There are 9 small triangles in the shape shown to the right. The shape is three triangles high.

How many small triangles would there be in a similar shape that's four triangles high?

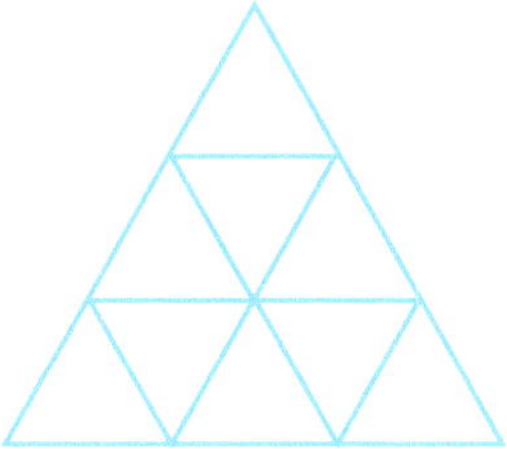

☐

19 Noah, Lucas, Jack and Henry all drove one lap around a go-kart track. They put their results in the table below.
Who drove the quickest?

Name	Time (seconds)
Noah	58.95
Lucas	59.01
Jack	59.9
Henry	57.99

Noah ☐ Lucas ☐ Jack ☐ Henry ☐

20 When your right foot goes around once on your bicycle pedal, the back wheel goes around one and a half times.

How many turns would the back wheel make if your right foot went around seven times?

- ☐ seven and half turns
- ☐ nine and half turns
- ☐ ten turns
- ☐ ten and half turns

21 Jonathan drove up the street to get some camping gear. The graph below shows the speed of his car during the time he was away.

How long after starting could he have bought the camping gear?

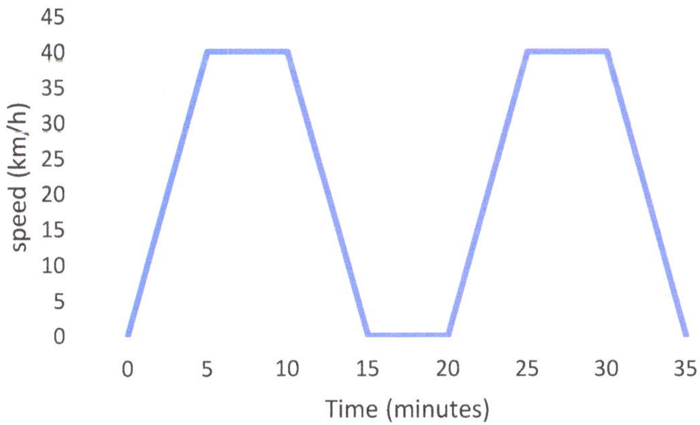

7 minutes	10 minutes	18 minutes	35 minutes
☐	☐	☐	☐

22 This rectangle covers 18 dots.

If I double each side of the rectangle, how many dots would the bigger rectangle cover?

36 ☐ 48 ☐ 54 ☐ 72 ☐

23 Class KB counted the vehicles that passed by the window during their maths lesson. They put the results in the following pictogram.

How many sedans and hatchbacks did they see in total?

SUV	
Sedan	
Coupe	
Hatchback	

= 4 vehicles

24 Find the difference between 3137 and 2784 after you have rounded them to the nearest hundred.

300 ☐ 400 ☐ 500 ☐ 600 ☐

NUMERACY YEAR 4

25 Ezra drew the following bar chart to show the favourite sports of children in his year group.

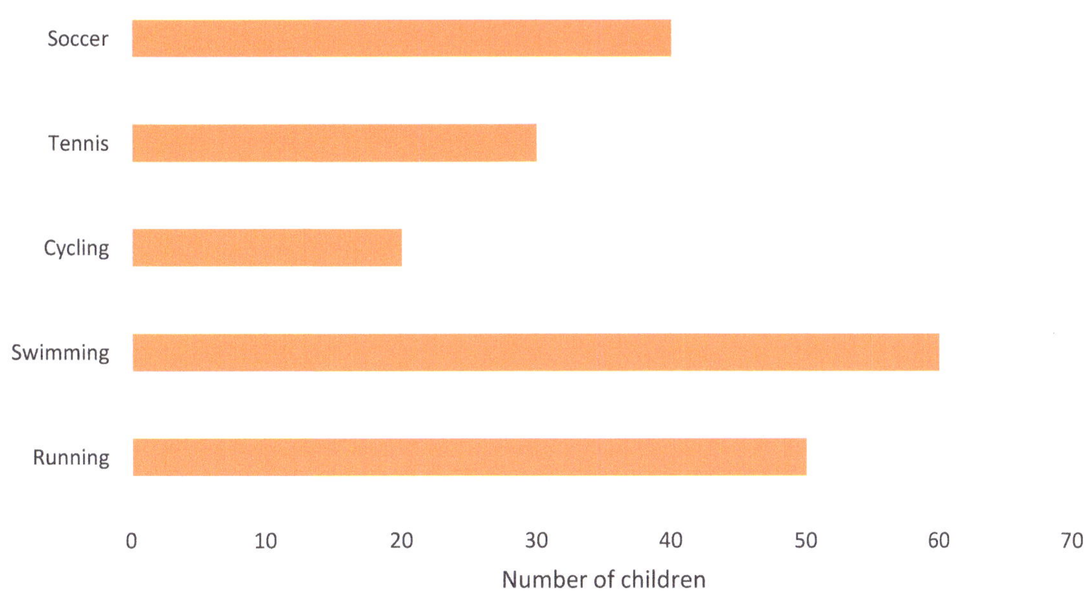

Soccer
Tennis
Cycling
Swimming
Running

0 10 20 30 40 50 60 70

Number of children

Which sport did fewest children choose?

26 In a game Team 1 scored 98 points, Team 2 scored 265, Team 3 scored 174 and Team 4 scored 189. The teams are sorted into Divisions 1 and 2, with Division 1 consisting of Team 1 and 2 and Division 2 consisting of Team 3 and 4. The Division with the highest number of points gets through to the next round.

Which of the following statements is true?

- ☐ Division 1 will go through to the next round.
- ☐ Division 2 will go through to the next round.
- ☐ It is a draw between Division 1 and 2.
- ☐ Team 4 and Team 1 together scored higher than Team 3 and Team 2 together.

27 Car A travels 30 km in 1 hour, Car B travels 60 km in 2 hours, Car C travels 120 km in 4 hours and Car D travels 200 km in 5 hours.

Which car has the highest average speed?

Car A ☐ Car B ☐ Car C ☐ Car D ☐

28 In my Year 4 class, there are 25 boys and 25 girls. 5 students are chess players. I placed all the names of my Year 4 class into a hat and then pulled one name out.

What are the chances that this student is a chess player?

Almost certain ☐ Impossible ☐ One chance in five ☐ One chance in ten ☐

29 How many edges does the prism below have?

15 ☐ 18 ☐ 20 ☐ 21 ☐

30 This chart shows how Mel spent time last Monday.

School
Sleep
Play
Eat
Homework

About how many hours did he spend on homework?

30 minutes ☐ 2 hours ☐ 3 hours ☐ 4 hours ☐

31 Twice an odd number, added to three times another odd number, makes 87. What are the numbers?

11 and 13 ☐ 17 and 20 ☐ 9 and 23 ☐ 15 and 12 ☐

32 I bought a case of 18 mangoes for $13.00.

Each mango cost about ☐

50 cents ☐ 70 cents ☐ 90 cents ☐ $1.10 ☐

33 Four judges gave the following scores to each of four contestants in a diving competition.

	Diver 1	Diver 2	Diver 3	Diver 4
Judge A	80	30	80	50
Judge B	90	75	70	90
Judge C	90	75	60	95
Judge D	80	95	90	85

A diver's final score is calculated by first removing the highest and lowest score then finding the sum of the remaining scores.

Which diver wins the competition?

Diver 1 ☐ Diver 2 ☐ Diver 3 ☐ Diver 4 ☐

34 Which of the following is **not** a tessellation?

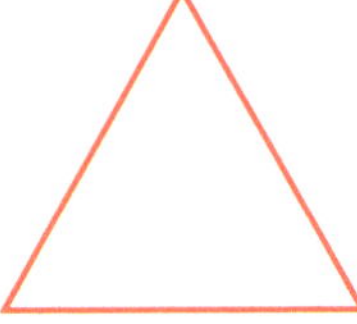 ☐
 ☐
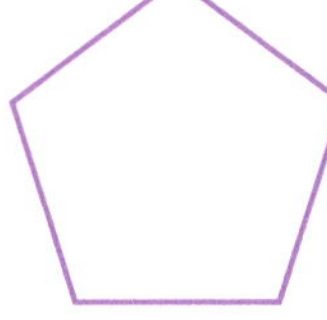 ☐
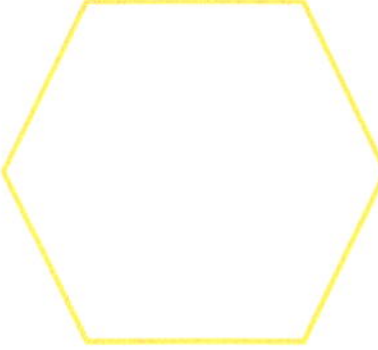 ☐

35 A crystal is growing in a solution. At 8:00 am its mass was 10 grams and its mass increased by 2.3 grams per hour.

What would be its weight at 6:00 pm on the same day?

☐ grams

36 Which one of the following is false?

- [ ] 0.1 is equivalent to 10%
- [ ] $\frac{7}{10}$ is equivalent to 70%
- [ ] 0.09 is equivalent to $\frac{9}{1000}$
- [ ] 25% is equivalent to $\frac{1}{4}$

37 When a bottle is half full of water it weighs 300 g.
When it is one quarter full, it weighs 250 g.
What is the weight of the bottle?

38 30 students were asked whether they played basketball or tennis.
The table below shows the results.

Plays basketball	Plays tennis	Plays both basketball and tennis	Plays neither basketball nor tennis
21	17	10	

How many students play neither basketball nor tennis?

39 The volume of the rectangular prism below is 112 cm^3. What is its height?

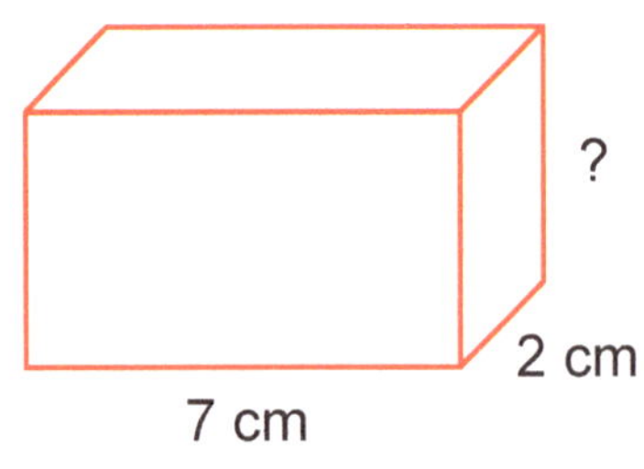

40 The timetable below shows the starting and finishing times of different sports games on television.

Game	Basketball	Soccer	Rugby	Tennis
Start	7:30 pm	7:55 pm	8:15 pm	8:25 pm
Finish	10:15 pm	10:25 pm	10:50 pm	11:00 pm

Peter has 150 minutes of recording time left on his camera.

Which whole game can he record?

Basketball ☐ Soccer ☐ Rugby ☐ Tennis ☐

Year 4 NAPLAN*-Format

NUMERACY PRACTICE TEST 3

Instructions

- There are 40 questions.
- You have 50 minutes to complete the test.
- You have to shade one bubble for each multiple-choice question.
- Write your answer in the box for short answer questions.

NAME : ______________________ **SCORE :_________**

1 Which of the following pairs of numbers are factors of 48?

8 and 9 ☐ 12 and 15 ☐ 12 and 24 ☐ 6 and 36 ☐

2 Jane buys some bags of biscuits for her dog.

There are 9 biscuits in each bag.

She gets 108 biscuits altogether. How many bags did she buy?

☐

3 A square is shown below.

The square above has been rotated anticlockwise into the position shown below.

Through what angle has the square been rotated anticlockwise?

90° ☐ 180° ☐ 270° ☐ 360° ☐

NUMERACY YEAR 4

The pie chart below shows how Daniel spent his weekly allowance of $180.

Use it to answer questions 4 and 5.

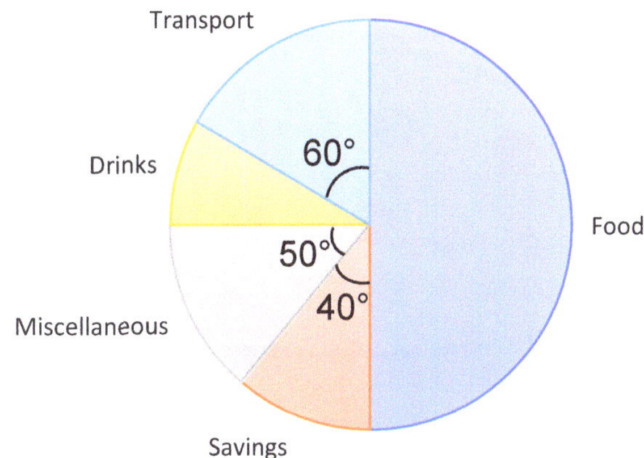

4 How much did he save?

$10 ▭ $20 ▭ $30 ▭ $40 ▭

5 How much did he spend on drinks?

$15 ▭ $25 ▭ $30 ▭ $35 ▭

6 I have a bag with 4 red balls, 5 blue balls and 7 yellow balls. If I pick one out at random, what is the probability that the ball is red?

- [ ] $\frac{1}{8}$
- [ ] $\frac{1}{4}$
- [ ] $\frac{5}{16}$
- [ ] $\frac{7}{16}$

7

The scores for hitting each part of the above target are:

Red	7 points
Yellow	5 points
Blue	3 points
Miss	0 points

George scored 17 points after three shots.

Where did his three arrows land?

- [ ] Red, Yellow, Blue
- [ ] Yellow, Yellow, Blue
- [ ] Blue, Blue, Red
- [ ] Blue, Red, Red

8 Harry lives 800 m from his school. He walks to and from school each day.

How far will he have walked travelling between home and school in 5 days?

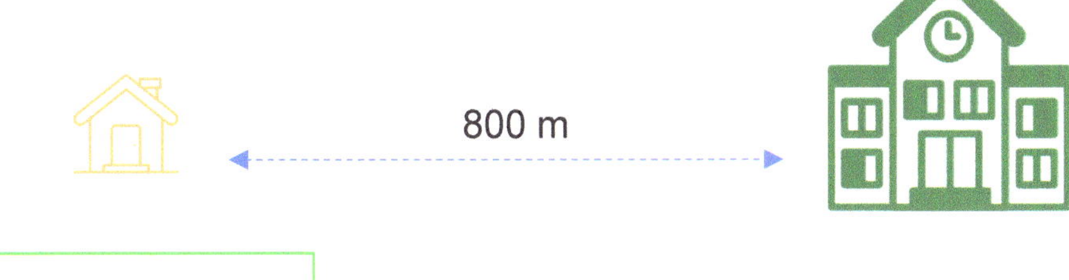

☐ km

9 Look at the function machine below.

If the number 25 comes out of the machine, what number went in?

☐

10 Mr William started filling in the table below to record the number of children from Year 4 and 5 who were going on a school trip.

How many Year 4 boys went on the trip?

	Year 4	Year 5	Total
Boys	?		72
Girls	42	43	
Total		70	

42	45	47	49
☐	☐	☐	☐

11 This shape is made from six identical rectangles.
What is the perimeter of the shape?

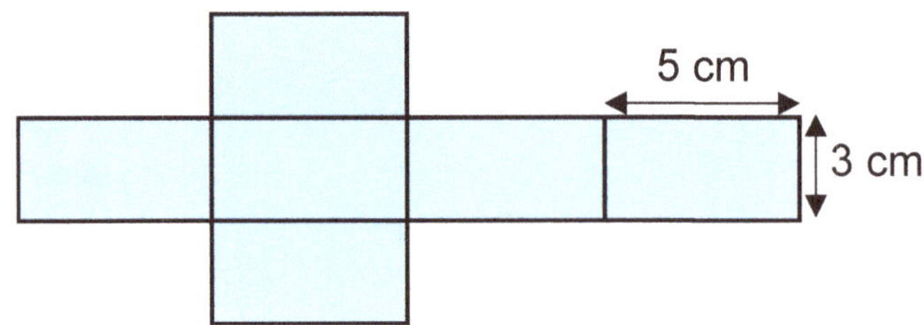

12 Below is a number pattern.

3	6	9	12	15	18	21	24	27	30
5	10	15	20	25	30	35	40	45	50
8	16	24	32	40	48	57	64	72	80

Which one of the numbers in the grid does **not** follow the pattern?

- ☐ 21
- ☐ 25
- ☐ 32
- ☐ 57

13 Arrange the following fractions in descending order.

$$\frac{6}{25}, \frac{3}{15}, \frac{6}{19}, \frac{6}{18}, \frac{6}{20}$$

- ☐ $\frac{3}{15}, \frac{6}{25}, \frac{6}{19}, \frac{6}{18}, \frac{6}{20}$
- ☐ $\frac{3}{15}, \frac{6}{18}, \frac{6}{19}, \frac{6}{20}, \frac{6}{25}$
- ☐ $\frac{6}{18}, \frac{6}{19}, \frac{6}{20}, \frac{6}{25}, \frac{3}{15}$
- ☐ $\frac{6}{25}, \frac{6}{20}, \frac{6}{19}, \frac{6}{18}, \frac{3}{15}$

14 The solid below is made up of 8 identical cubes.

The volume of the solid is 125 cm^3.

Find the length of one side of each cube.

1.5 cm ☐ 2 cm ☐ 2.5 cm ☐ 5 cm ☐

15 $3 \times \square = 4 \times 9 + 18 \div 6$

Which number should be in the box to make this number sentence true?

12 ☐ 13 ☐ 14 ☐ 15 ☐

16 What is the missing fraction on the number line shown below?

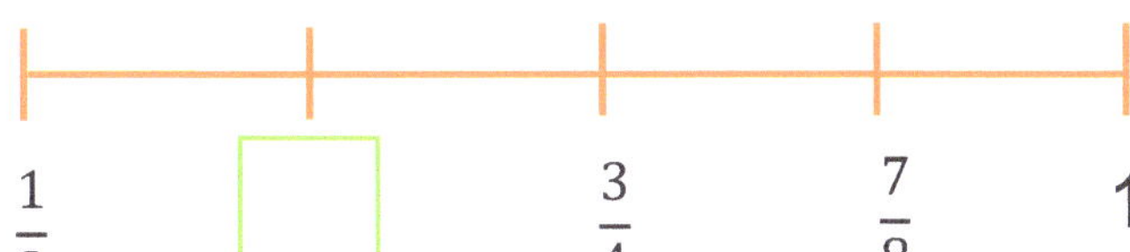

$\frac{1}{2}$ ☐ $\frac{3}{4}$ $\frac{7}{8}$ 1

17 How many of the numbers shown below are both multiples of 8 and 9?

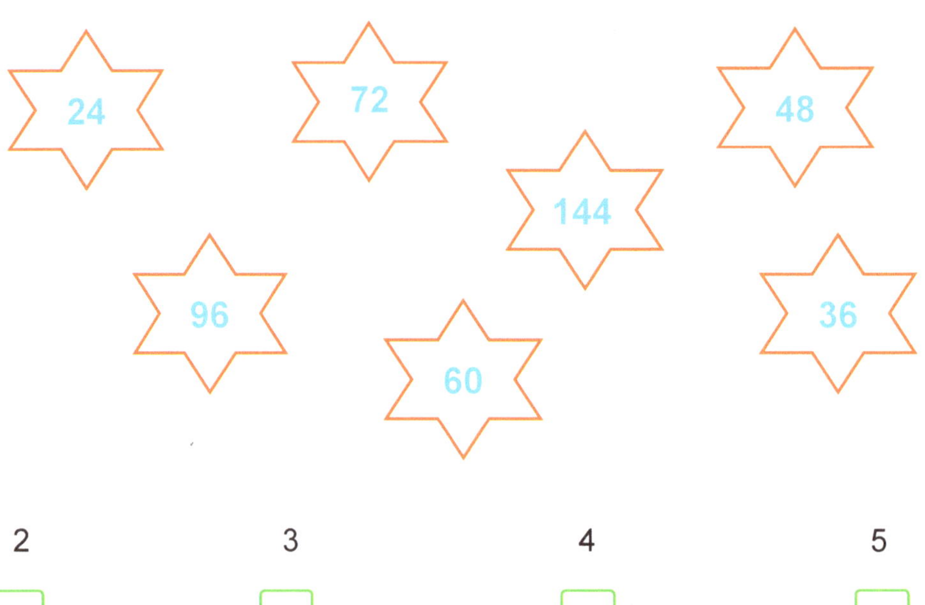

2 ☐ 3 ☐ 4 ☐ 5 ☐

18 Find the missing digit in the multiplication below.

```
      1 9 4
  ×     3 ?
  ---------
    1 7 4 6
    5 8 2 0
  ---------
    7 5 6 6
```

? = ☐

19 After reading $\frac{1}{7}$ of a book on the first day and another $\frac{2}{7}$ of it on the second day, Mrs James has 96 pages left. How many pages are there in the book?

☐

NUMERACY YEAR 4

20 The graph below shows the number of books some Year 4 students read in a week.

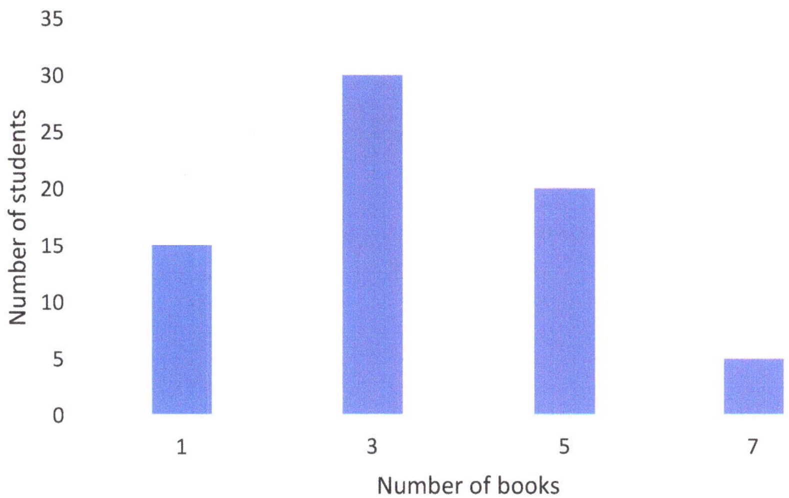

How many students read less than 3 books in a week?

21 Sally had 6 five-dollar notes. She changed them for twenty-cent coins.

How many coins did she get?

22 When a container is half-filled with rice, it weighs 2 kg 960 g. If the mass of the empty container is 560 g, how much more rice is needed to fill up the container completely?

☐ kg

23 What fraction of the figure below is shaded?

$\frac{1}{2}$ ☐ $\frac{4}{9}$ ☐ $\frac{5}{9}$ ☐ $\frac{7}{18}$ ☐

24 Which of these is equal to 150?

- ☐ 151 to the nearest 100
- ☐ 149.4 to the nearest whole number
- ☐ 146 to the nearest 10
- ☐ 155 to the nearest 10

NUMERACY YEAR 4

25 The table below shows the favourite food of some students in a college.

Food	Noodles	Pizza	Hot Dog	Burger
Number of Students	45	35	?	28

130 students were involved in the survey.

How many students like hot dogs?

22 ☐ 24 ☐ 26 ☐ 28 ☐

26 The graph below shows the number of people who visited the Royal Botanic Gardens in a certain week.

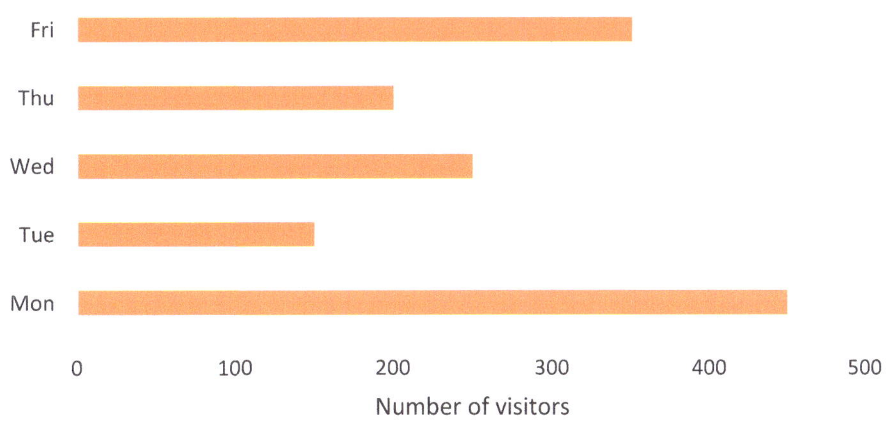

The day with the highest number of visitors was ☐

27 What is the HCF of 18 and 12?

3 ☐ 6 ☐ 9 ☐ 12 ☐

28 Adrian had 1 hour and 45 min to complete his school work. He started at 2:50 pm and finished at 4:45 pm.

How much extra time did he take?

- [ ] 5 minutes
- [ ] 10 minutes
- [ ] 15 minutes
- [ ] 20 minutes

29 There are eight squares, each 4 m by 4 m, placed side by side as shown below. What is the total area of the 8 squares?

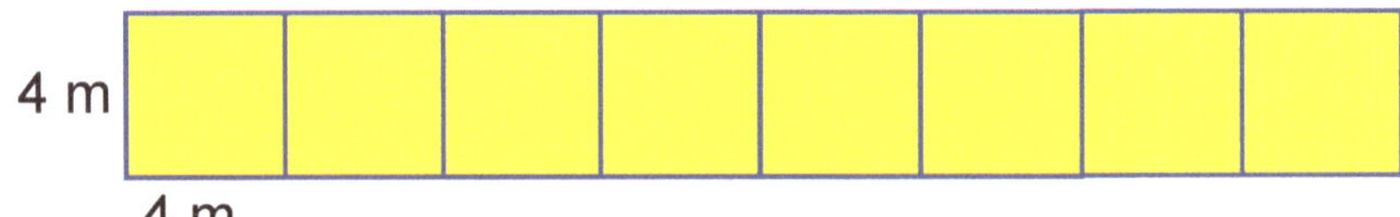

[ ]

30 Jason bought 2 L of paint. He used $\frac{3}{4}$ L to paint a fence and $\frac{1}{6}$ L to paint a door. How much paint had he left?

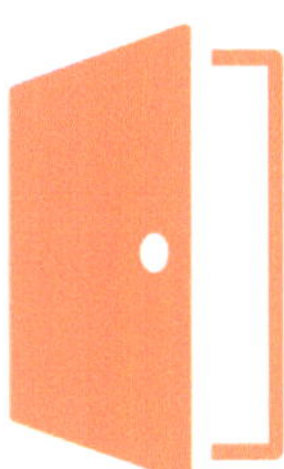

[ ] L

31 In the figure below, ∠ e is

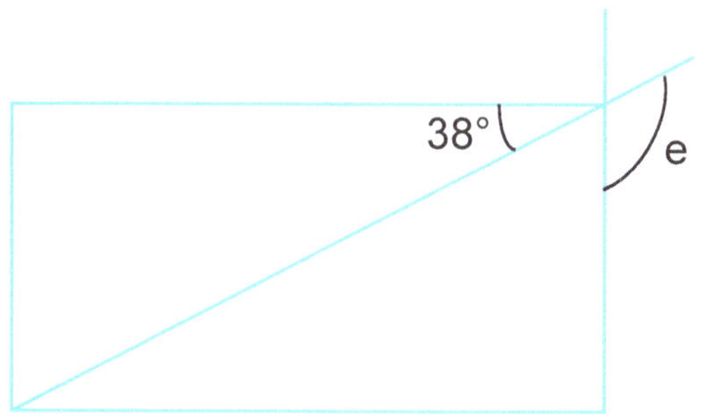

38°

e

52° 118° 128° 138°

32 Which one of the following statements is true?

- A pentagonal pyramid has five faces.
- A triangle-based pyramid has one square face.
- A pentagonal prism has five pentagonal faces.
- A triangular prism has two triangular faces.

33 The arrow on the spinner below is spun once.

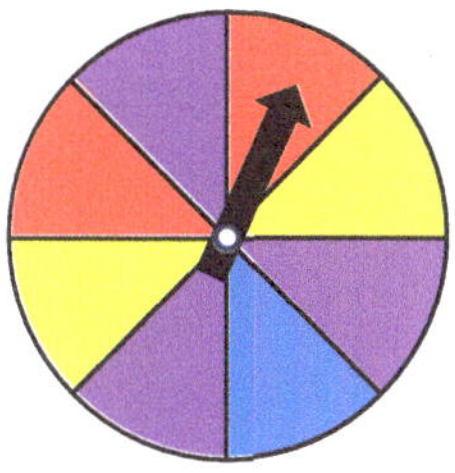

What is the chance of obtaining red?

- 1 chance in 2
- 1 chance in 3
- 1 chance in 4
- 1 chance in 8

34 How many right angles altogether are in this square?

4 ☐ 8 ☐ 12 ☐ 16 ☐

35 How many axes of symmetry does this shape have?

1 ☐ 2 ☐ 4 ☐ 8 ☐

36 An airplane was flying in a north-westly direction. It turned around and headed in the opposite direction.

In which direction was it then flying?

south-west ☐ south-east ☐ north-east ☐ north-west ☐

Questions 37 and 38 refer to the graph below.

This graph shows Julia's distance from home at each hour on a shopping trip.

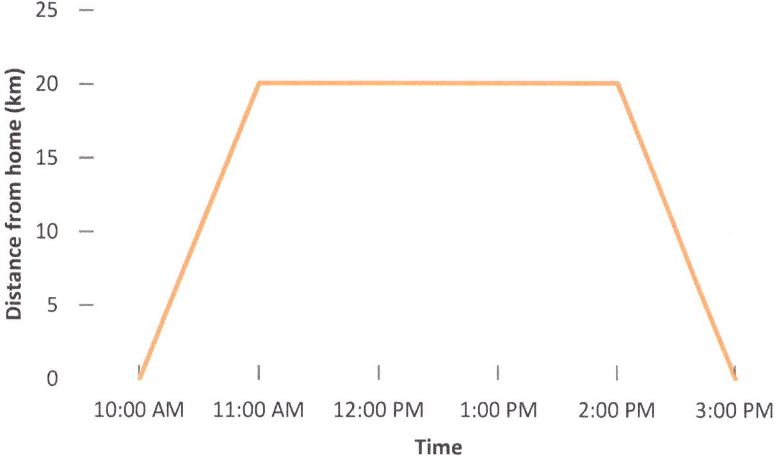

37 What was the total distance travelled by Julia on her journey?

10 km ☐ 20 km ☐ 30 km ☐ 40 km ☐

38 What was the average speed for Julia's return journey?

10 km/h ☐ 20 km/h ☐ 30 km/h ☐ 40 km/h ☐

Use the following information to answer questions 39 and 40.

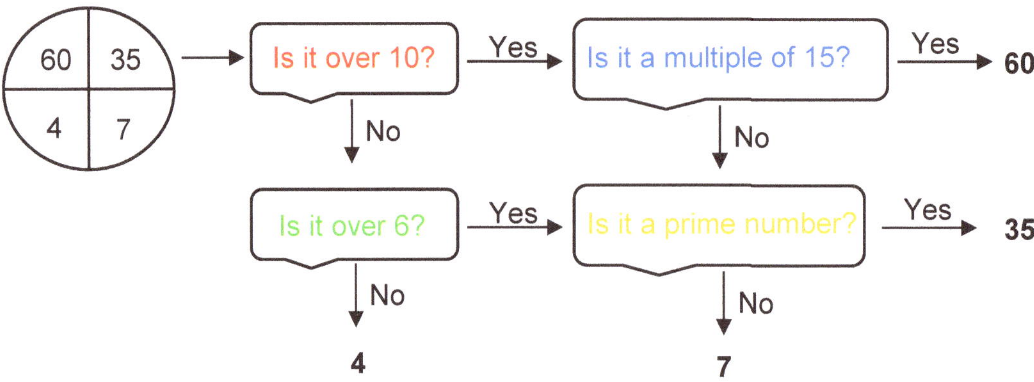

39 Which question is **incorrect**?

- Is it over 10?
- Is it a multiple of 15?
- Is it over 6?
- Is it a prime number?

40 Which question should replace the incorrect question?

- Is it a multiple of 2?
- Is it a factor of 15?
- Is it a composite number?
- Is it less than 10?

Year 4 NAPLAN*-Format

NUMERACY PRACTICE TEST 4

Instructions

- There are 40 questions.
- You have 50 minutes to complete the test.
- You have to shade one bubble for each multiple-choice question.
- Write your answer in the box for short answer questions.

NAME : ____________________ **SCORE :**__________

1 Find the difference between ninety tens and twenty hundreds.

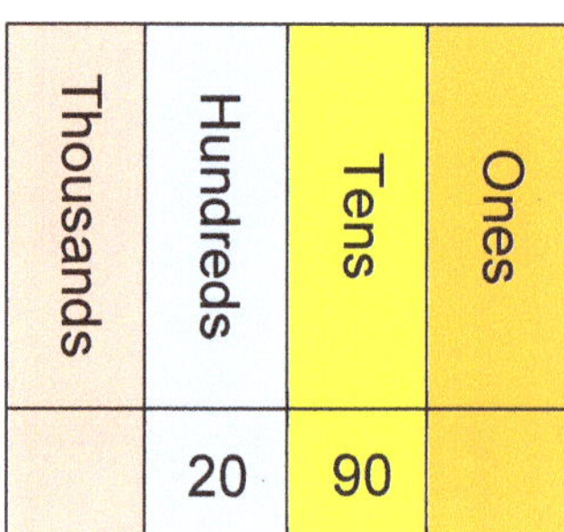

2900	1100	700	70
☐	☐	☐	☐

2 Find the quotient when 6864 is divided by 22.

$$22\overline{)6864}$$

312	321	322	324
☐	☐	☐	☐

3 If you can only travel along the arrows and in the direction of the arrows, how many different ways are there to get from home to library?

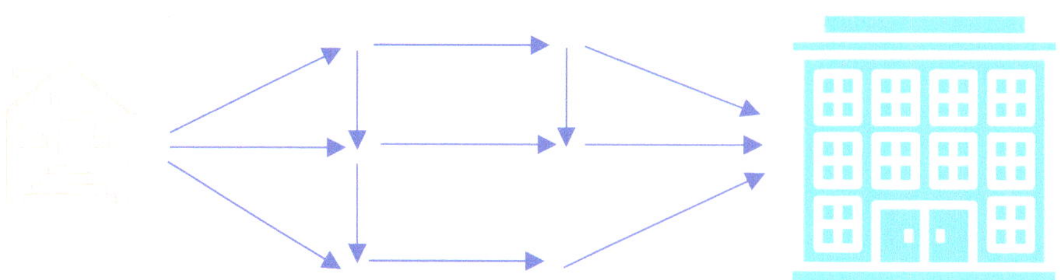

5	6	7	8
☐	☐	☐	☐

4 Here is a shape made of squares.

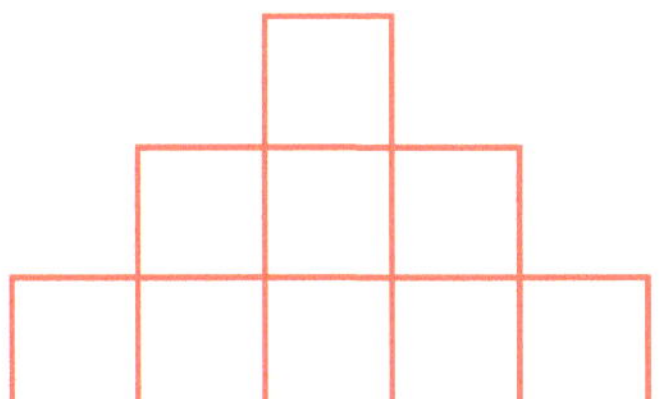

If the total area is 36 cm^2, what is the perimeter?

- [ ] 32 cm
- [ ] 34 cm
- [ ] 36 cm
- [ ] 38 cm

5 George can eat 10 lollies in an hour. His brother can eat the same amount in 2 hours.

How long will it take both of them together to eat 15 lollies?

- [ ] 30 minutes
- [ ] 45 minutes
- [ ] 1 hour
- [ ] 2 hours

6 How many prime numbers are below?

- [ ] 2
- [ ] 3
- [ ] 4
- [ ] 5

7 The table below shows a weather report for four days.

Day	Lowest Temperature	Highest Temperature
Monday	1°C	10°C
Tuesday	0°C	9°C
Wednesday	−2°C	8°C
Thursday	−3°C	0°C

During which day did the temperature change the most?

Monday ☐ Tuesday ☐ Wednesday ☐ Thursday ☐

8 Bees have 6 legs. Spiders have 8 legs.
Harry saw a picture of spiders and bees and counted 50 legs altogether.

How many spiders did Harry see in the picture?

3 ☐ 4 ☐ 5 ☐ 6 ☐

9 How many edges does the 3D object below have?

6 ☐ 8 ☐ 12 ☐ 16 ☐

10 In a group of 25 students there were some who played soccer only, some who played cricket only and some who played both.

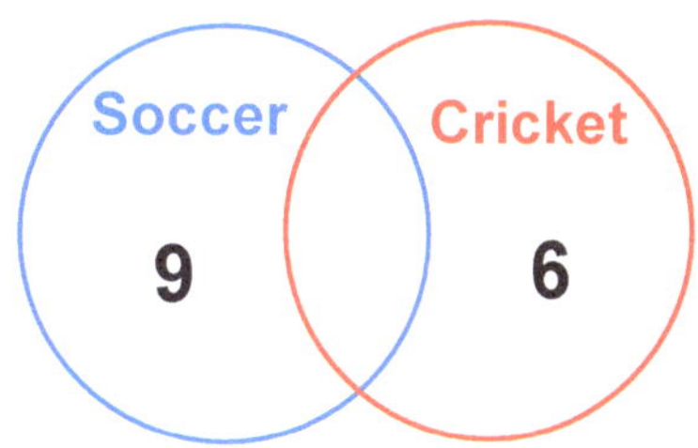

How many students played both soccer and cricket?

10 ☐ 15 ☐ 18 ☐ 20 ☐

11 Which 3D object has the following views?

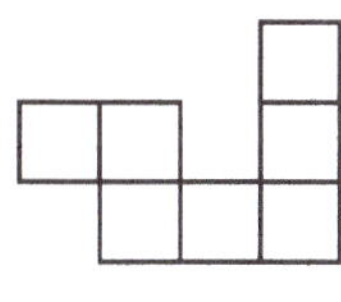
Top

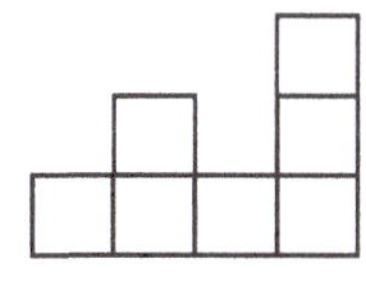
Front

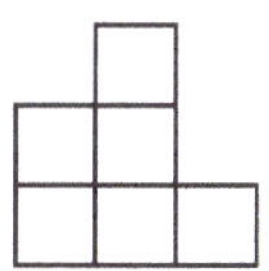
Side

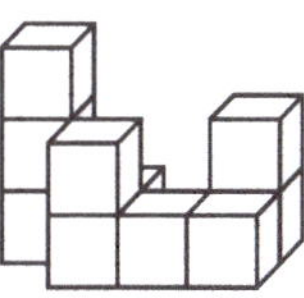 ☐

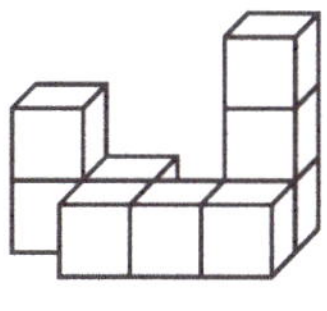 ☐

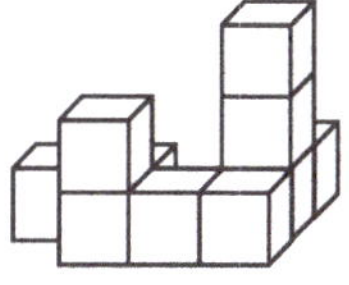 ☐

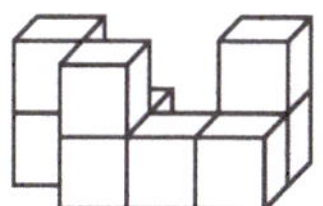 ☐

12 Mark built a fence around his garden.

6 m

6 m

How long was the fence?

[ ]

13 A student squares a number. The answer ends in a 9.
Which of the following statements is true?

- [ ] The original number could have ended in a 3 and a 6.
- [ ] The original number could have ended in a 6 and a 9.
- [ ] The original number could have ended in a 3 and a 7.
- [ ] The original number could have ended in a 7 and a 9.

14 Consider the three digits below.

7 3 9

3-digit numbers can be formed using the above digits.

What is the difference between the largest number and the smallest number?

[ ]

15 Imagine that we are slicing a square pyramid. Depending on which direction we cut, we will get different cross-sections.

Which one of the followings could **not** be the cross-section of a square pyramid?

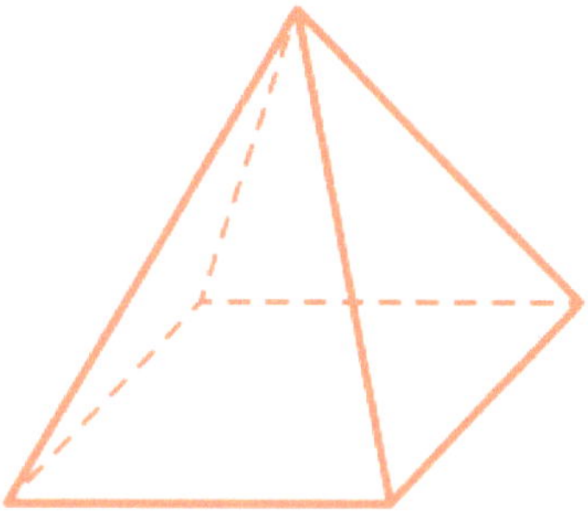

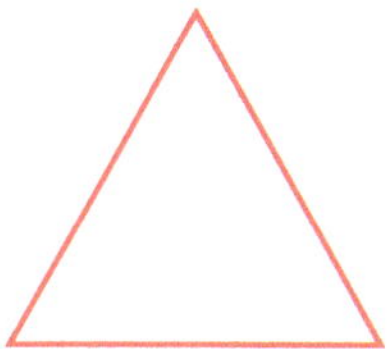

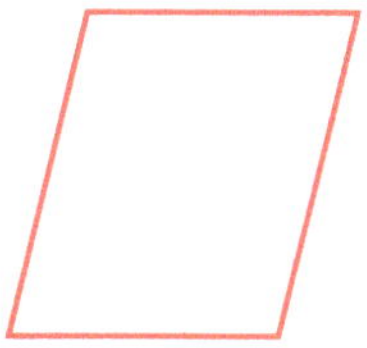

☐ ☐ ☐ ☐

16 Eric spent all of his pocket money on food, toys, lollies and books. He spent the most money on toys. Which graph shows this?

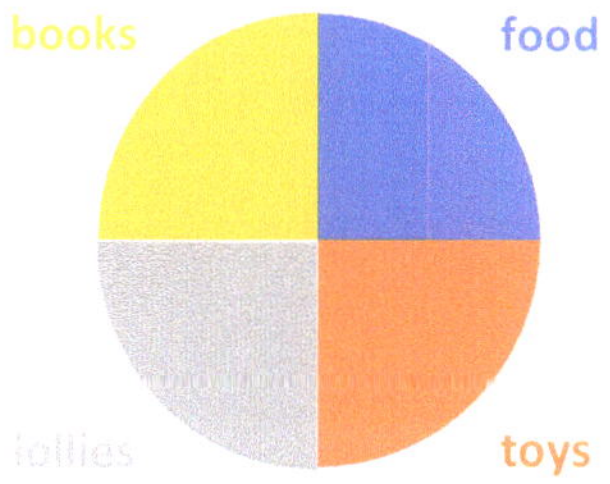

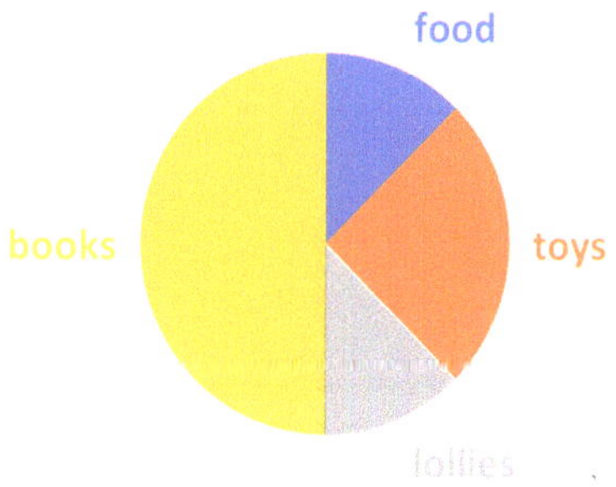

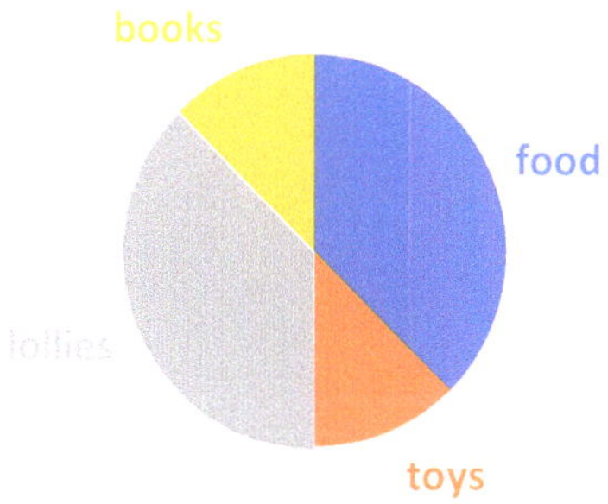

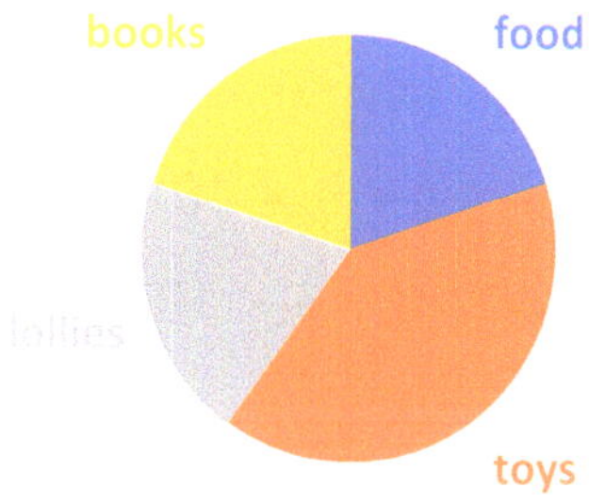

☐

☐

☐

☐

17 The table below shows the postage rates for sending parcels to Canada.

Mass step not over	Postage
1 kg	$12.00
2 kg	$18.00
5 kg	$35.00
Per additional step of 1 kg	$5.00

Find the postage for a parcel of mass 13 kg.

- [ ] $40.00
- [ ] $55.00
- [ ] $70.00
- [ ] $75.00

18 Jayden has a job mowing a golf course. He hires a mower for $150 and is paid a total of $300 for the job. If it takes him 6 hours, how much per hour was he paid?

19 Which one of the following expressions equals 84?

- [ ] $3 \times (8 + 6) \times 10$
- [ ] $3 \times 8 + 6 \times 10$
- [ ] $3 \times (8 + 6 \times 10)$
- [ ] $(3 \times 8 + 6) \times 10$

20 In a relay race where the competitors swim until they are tired, Vince swam 3.5 km, Bennie swam 5.2 km and Daniel swam 3.9 km.

What is the average distance they swam?

[ ] km

21 The total height of a tree is 5 m.
If a quarter of the tree is below ground, how much will be above ground?

3.75 m	360 cm	460 cm	3.8 m
☐	☐	☐	☐

22 Lewis purchased a jacket for 75% off its original price. If he paid with a $100 note and received $55 change, how much was the jacket originally?

75% off

[ ]

23 Which of the following is **not** equal to three-quarters of a number?

- ☐ the number divided by 4 then multiplied by 3
- ☐ the whole number minus 25% of the number
- ☐ the number divided by 75 then multiplied by 100
- ☐ 75% of the number

24 Vivian went shopping and purchased 5 kg of sweet potatoes at $6.00/kg, 0.5 kg of mushrooms at $18.40/kg, and 1.4 kg of onions at $3.00/kg.
She paid at the checkout with a credit card.
How much was debited on her card?

$6.00/kg **$18.40/kg** **$3.00/kg**

☐

25 A tin full of biscuits has a mass of 1.73 kg. The mass of the empty tin is 550 g.

What is the net mass of the biscuits?

550 g

☐ kg

NUMERACY YEAR 4

26 Which of the following represents the best value for money?

- [ ] 100 g for $3.20
- [ ] 0.5 kg for $12.30
- [ ] 250 g for $8.10
- [ ] 1.5 kg for $33.60

27 In a rhombus, opposite angles are the same size.

If one angle is 117° as shown below, what is the size of angle x?

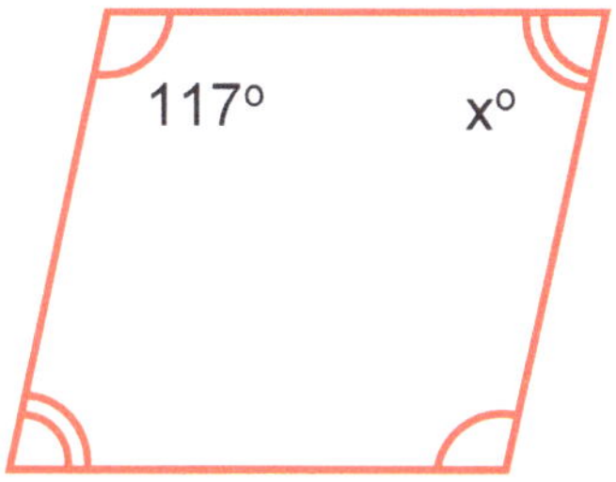

117°

x°

28 There are 4 red boxes in a green box. There are also 3 green boxes in a blue box. How many red boxes are there if there are 12 blue boxes?

Questions 29 and 30 refer to the following graph.

The graph below shows the favourite sports of a class of students in Year 4.

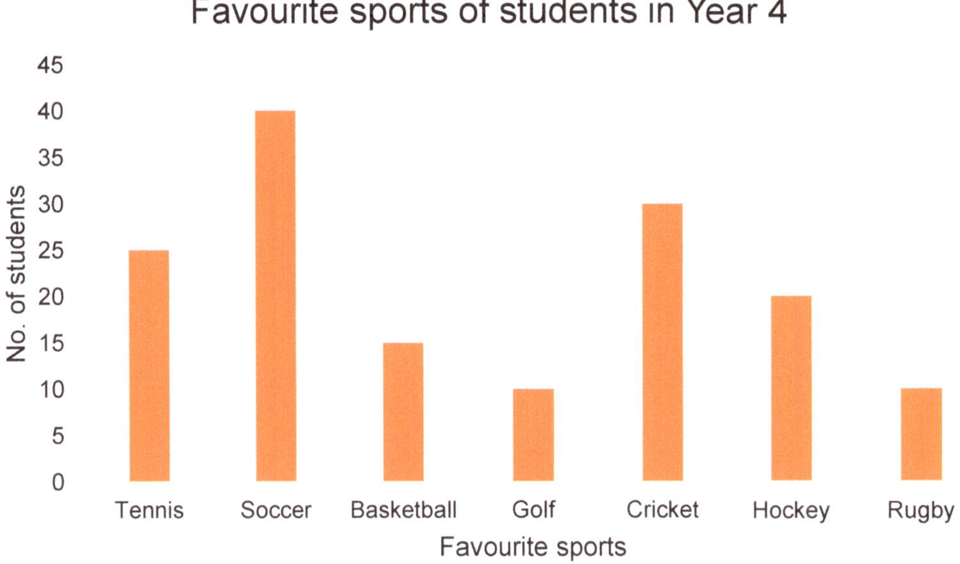

29 What is the probability of picking a student whose favourite sport is either hockey or golf?

15% ☐ 20% ☐ 25% ☐ 30% ☐

30 What is the difference between the probabilities of picking a student whose favourite sport is cricket and the probability of picking a student whose favourite sport is basketball?

5% ☐ 10% ☐ 15% ☐ 20% ☐

31

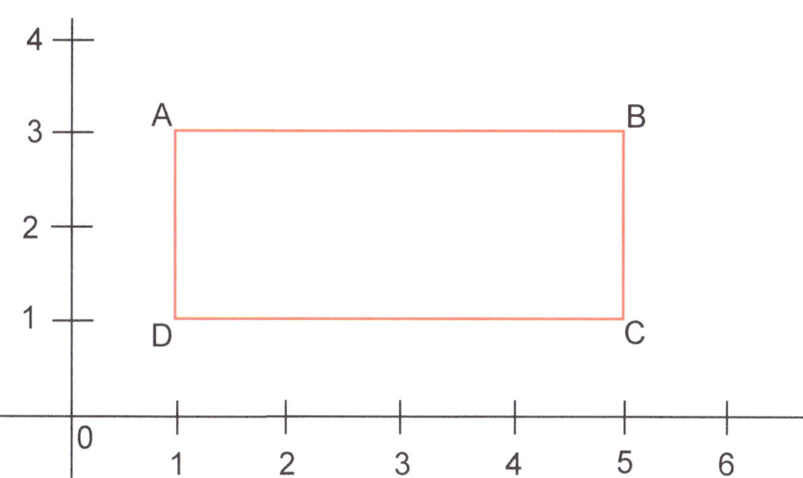

What are the coordinates of the point that is half-way between A and C?

(2, 2) ☐ (2, 3) ☐ (3, 2) ☐ (3, 3) ☐

32 The figure below is made of small cubes.
All surfaces of this figure are painted red.

How many faces on the small cubes have been painted red?

20 ☐ 22 ☐ 24 ☐ 28 ☐

33 Dennis is facing north and Andrew is facing south. Dennis makes a quarter turn to his right, while Andrew makes a quarter turn to his left.

Which one of the following statements is TRUE?

- ☐ Dennis is now facing West.
- ☐ They are facing the same direction.
- ☐ Dennis is facing the opposite direction from Andrew.
- ☐ Andrew is a quarter turn to the right of Dennis.

34 What is the area of the shaded part of following shape?

18 cm

4 cm

7 cm

11 cm

$168\ cm^2$	$170\ cm^2$	$198\ cm^2$	$216\ cm^2$
☐	☐	☐	☐

35 Lisa has drawn a pentagon.
She reflects her shape on the dotted mirror line shown to make a new shape.
What type of shape does she form?

pentagon	hexagon	heptagon	octagon
☐	☐	☐	☐

NUMERACY YEAR 4

36 Which statement below is **not** true about the spinner on the right?

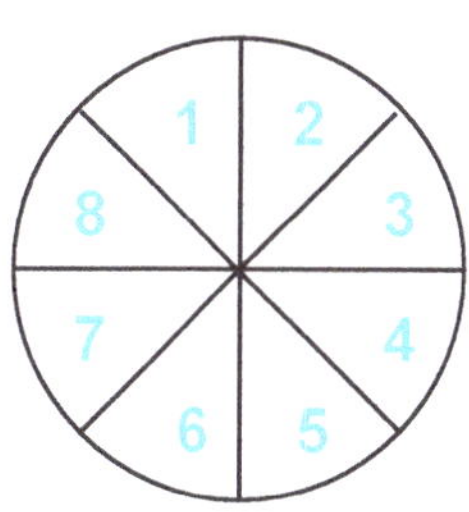

- [ ] It is equally likely to land on an odd or even number.
- [ ] There is an even chance of it landing on a number greater than 3.
- [ ] The probability of it landing on 5 is $\frac{1}{8}$.
- [ ] The probability of it landing on a number less than 2 is $\frac{1}{8}$.

37 Gwen is investigating a pattern of shapes made of squares as shown below.

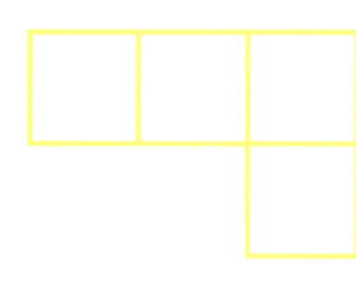
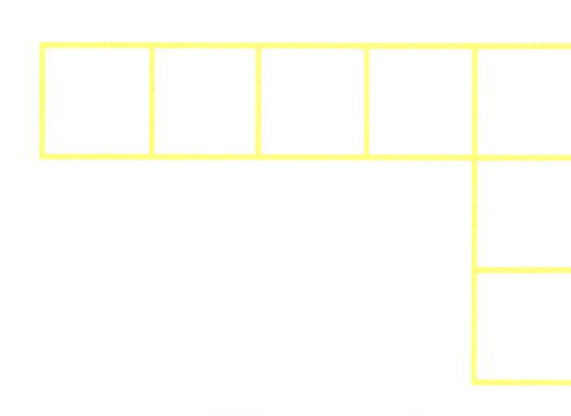

Shape 1 Shape 2 Shape 3

How many squares will be in the shape 7 of the pattern?

[ ]

38 John visited Sunshine Zoo on Monday 23rd January. He arrived 30 minutes after the zoo opened and left $1\frac{1}{2}$ hours before it closed.

How long did he stay there?

Sunshine Zoo Opening Hours	
June – August	September – May
9:30 am – 4:30 pm	9:30 am – 5:00 pm

[ ] hours

39 This shape is made up of identical regular hexagons. The perimeter of the shape is 72 cm. How long is each side of the hexagons?

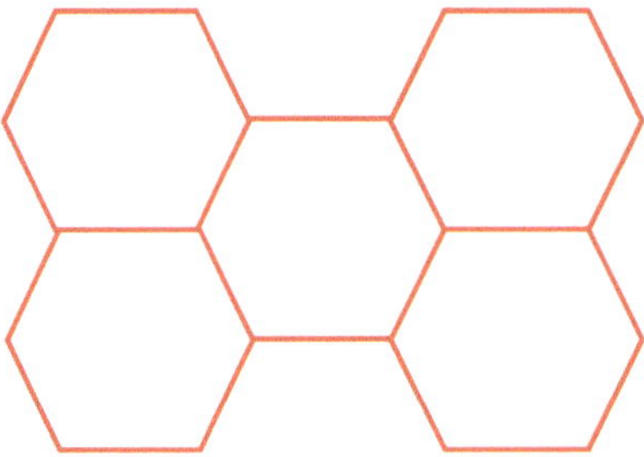

40 Clair's birthday is 20 days after Peter's. Peter celebrates his birthday on the 15th July. What date is Clair's birthday?

July						
SUN	MON	TUE	WED	THU	FRI	SAT
					1	2
3	4	5	6	7	8	9
10	11	12	13	14	15	16
17	18	19	20	21	22	23
24	25	26	27	28	29	30
31						

Year 4 NAPLAN*-Format

NUMERACY PRACTICE TEST 5

Instructions

- There are 40 questions.
- You have 50 minutes to complete the test.
- You have to shade one bubble for each multiple-choice question.
- Write your answer in the box for short answer questions.

NAME : ____________________ **SCORE :**__________

1 Isaac walked four times around the edges of a square field. Through how many right angles possibly did Isaac turn?

4 ☐ 8 ☐ 12 ☐ 16 ☐

2 Which one of these shapes is a quadrilateral?

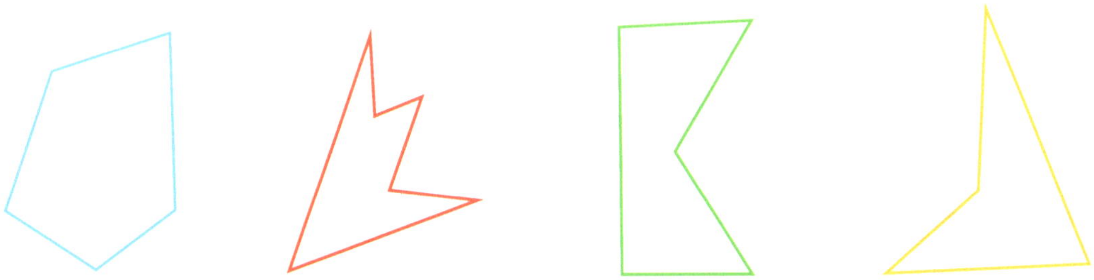

☐ ☐ ☐ ☐

3 If the figure below is a regular pentagon with a centre at A, what is the measure of the indicated angle?

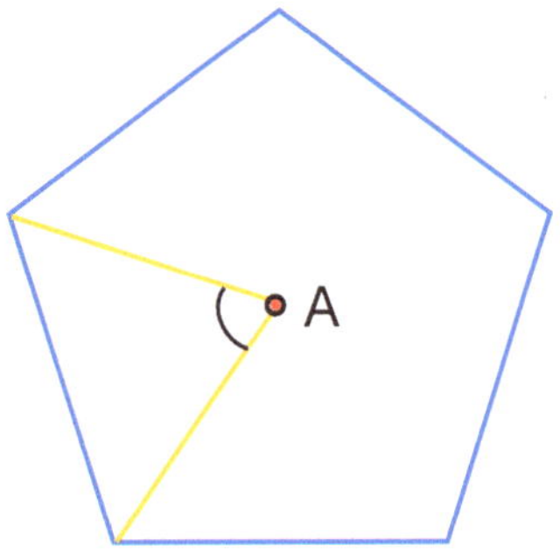

A

60° ☐ 68° ☐ 72° ☐ 80° ☐

4 What is the perimeter of the figure shown below?

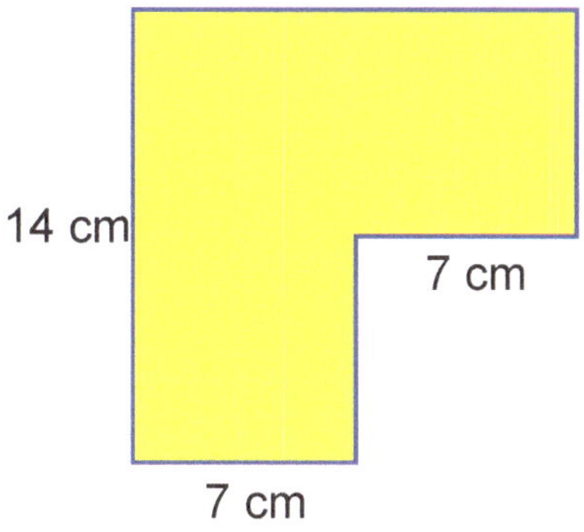

14 cm
7 cm
7 cm

☐

5 Liam drew an arrow pointing north below.

Which of these arrows is pointing south-east?

☐ ☐ ☐ ☐

6 A 300-page book is 3 centimetres thick.

What is the thickness of each page?

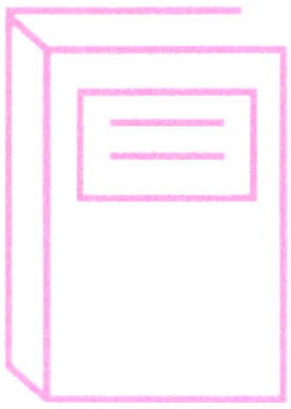

1 mm	0.1 mm	0.001 cm	0.0001 cm
☐	☐	☐	☐

7 Olivia counted the animals in a farm. She noticed that there were only four types. In total, Olivia recorded 100 animals.

She represented the results in the graph below.

chicken	goat	sheep	cow

How many sheep did Olivia record?

30 ☐ 50 ☐ 70 ☐ 90 ☐

8 Ian is saving money to buy a new skateboard. In the first month he saved $10. Every month after the first he saved $5 more than the month before.
How much money did Ian save in total in 4 months?

$40 ☐ $50 ☐ $60 ☐ $70 ☐

9 A group of students working on a school project recorded how many units of work they completed every day. They showed the data in the graph below.

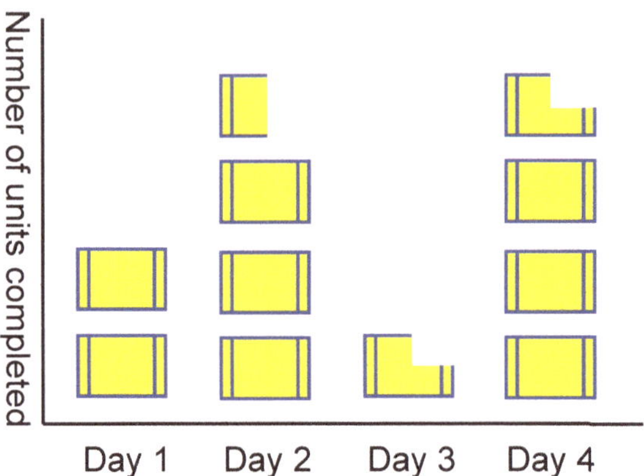

In total, the students completed 40 units of work.
How many units of work did they complete in the first two days?

10 Alan, Alex and Aiden took turns to paint their house. The house painting began at 8 am and finished at 8 pm without a break.

Aiden painted for one-quarter of the time. Alan painted for the same amount of time as Alex.

How long did Alex spend painting the house?

11 Use the following pie chart to answer the question.

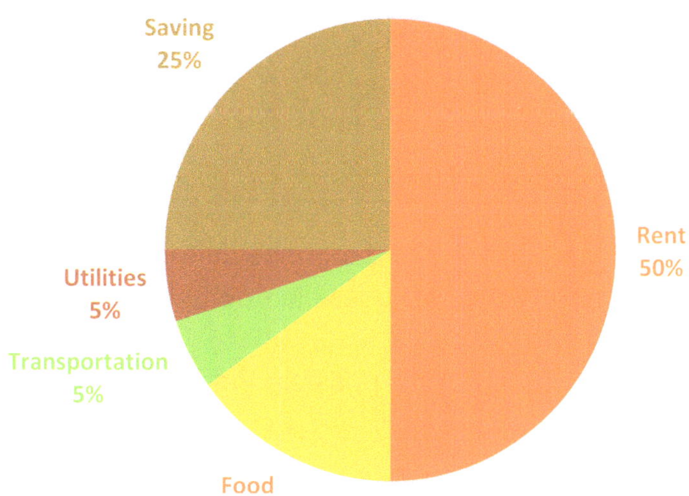

If Karen's monthly income is $4,000, how much does she spend on food each month?

12 Emma, Ava, Evelyn and Flora went to a fair.

Emma had $20 and spent $17.00.
Ava had $10 and spent $8.00.
Evelyn had $15 and spent $12.00.
Flora had $5 and spent $4.

Which girl spent the largest fraction of the money she had?

Emma ☐ Ava ☐ Evelyn ☐ Flora ☐

13 All the times shown on the clocks below were on the same day.

6:50 am	15:45	4:30 pm	16:05
A	**B**	**C**	**D**

What is the order of the clocks from the earliest time to the latest time?

A, B, C, D ☐ A, C, B, D ☐ A, B, D, C ☐ C, A, B, D ☐

14 Margaret uses only the digits 1 and 2 to make different three-digit numbers. For example, 121 and 111 are two possible numbers.

What is the sum of all of Margaret's possible three-digit numbers?

121 111 212 ...

922 ☐ 1091 ☐ 1121 ☐ 1332 ☐

15 Peter is at a theme park waiting in a queue for a vintage car ride.
Every 5 minutes, a car with 4 people leaves.
A car leaves and Peter counts 28 people ahead of him in the queue.
How many minutes will Peter have to wait until his car leaves?

- [ ] 25 minutes
- [ ] 30 minutes
- [ ] 35 minutes
- [ ] 40 minutes

16 Four children collected shells on a beach. They put their shells in piles as shown.

Child	Number of shells collected	Number of shells in each pile
Elia	36	3
Murphy	48	8
Clover	55	5
Della	60	4

Who made the largest number of piles?

[ ]

17 Elana looked at the clock as shown to the right as she left home for her afternoon swimming training.

She finished 1 hour 30 minutes later.

What time did Elana finish?

[ ]

Questions 18 and 19 refer to the following graph.

The bar graph below shows the number of books read by all the students in Primary 4B during the weekends.

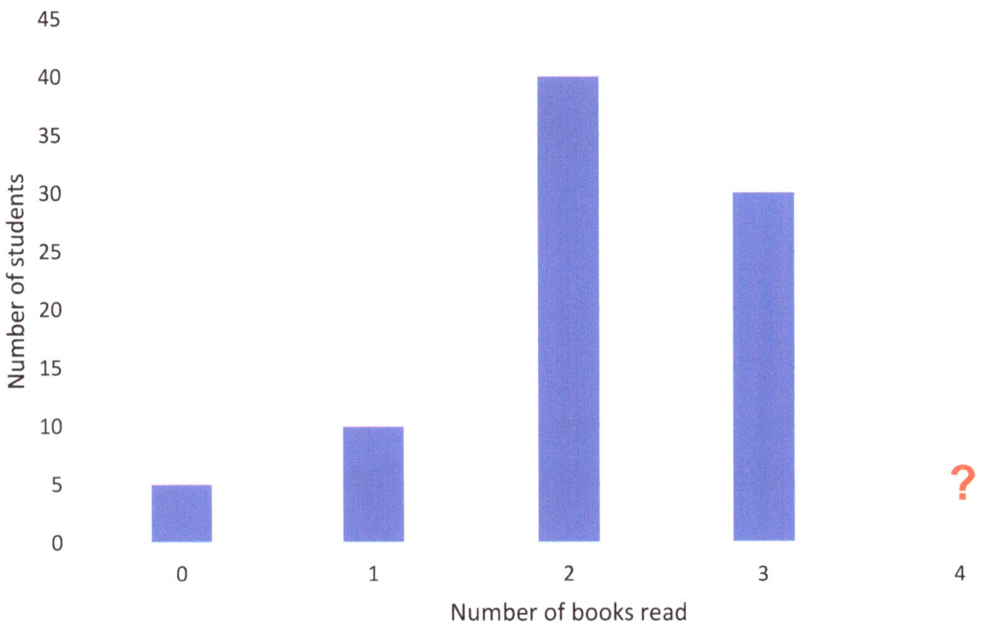

18 The students read a total of 200 books during the weekends.
How many students read 4 books during the weekends?

- 5
- 10
- 15
- 20

19 Find the difference between the number of students who read **less than 2 books** and the number of students who read **more than 2 books**.

20 Tara made a tally chart to show how many silver coins she has as shown below.

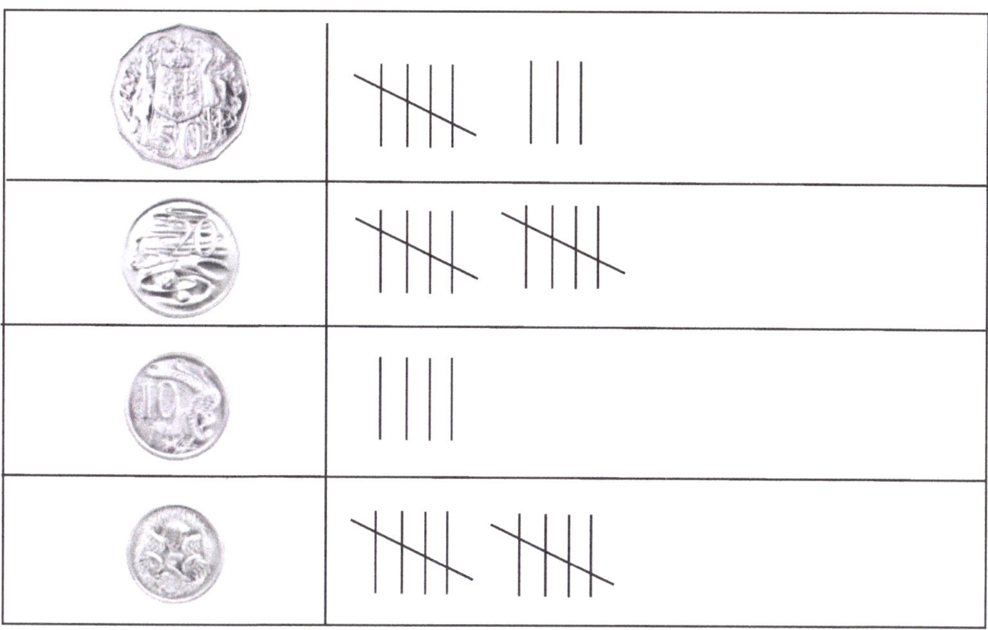

What is the total value of Tara's silver coins?

21 Sunny has the following shapes on a plate.

Sunny picked out two squares and didn't replace them.

What is the chance of picking a square on her third pick without looking?

- 20% ☐
- 25% ☐
- 33.3% ☐
- 50% ☐

22 Calculate the value of □.

$$7 + \frac{2}{\square} \times 24 = 15$$

3   4   6   9

23 Which 3D object has the following views?

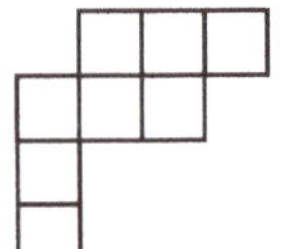

Top

Front

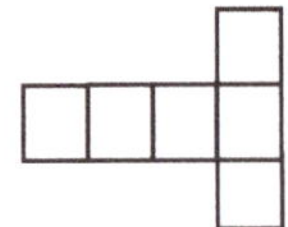

Side

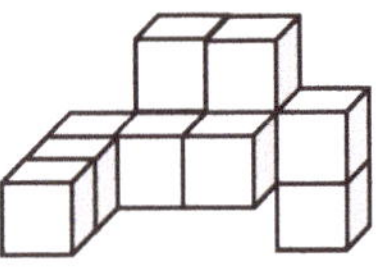

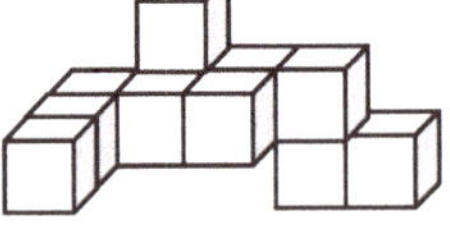

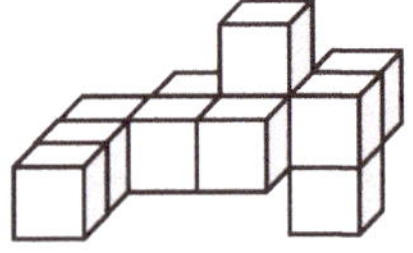

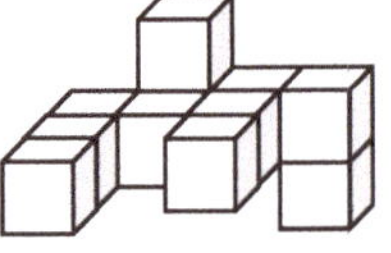

24 The following figure was dipped into a bucket of blue paint.

How many small cubes have one blue face?

4   6   8   12

Use the following information to answer questions 25 and 26.

The symbols produce the numbers as shown. If these processes were then arranged into a flowchart as shown below,

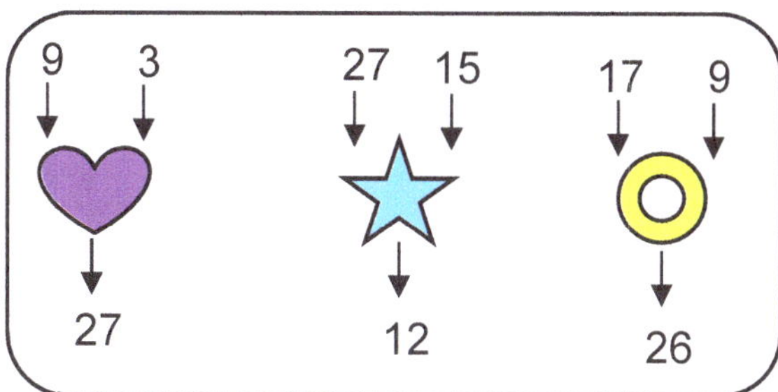

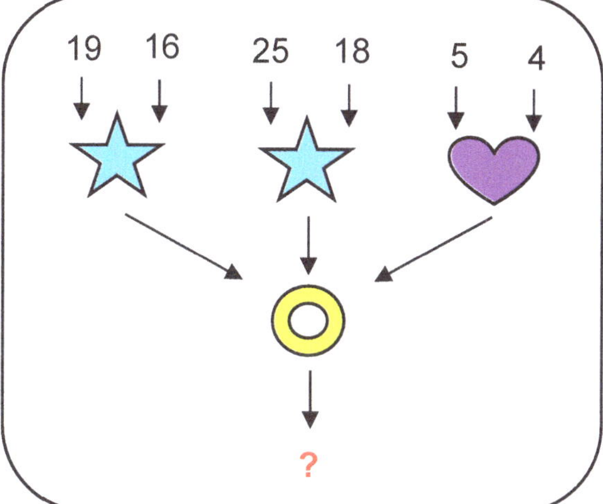

25 What is the output of the star in the middle?

26 What number should replace the question mark?

27 There are 420 people at the book fair. $\frac{3}{7}$ of them are children. $\frac{1}{3}$ of the remainder are men. How many women are there?

☐ women

28 The arrow is rotated 90 degrees clockwise and then reflected about the dotted line.

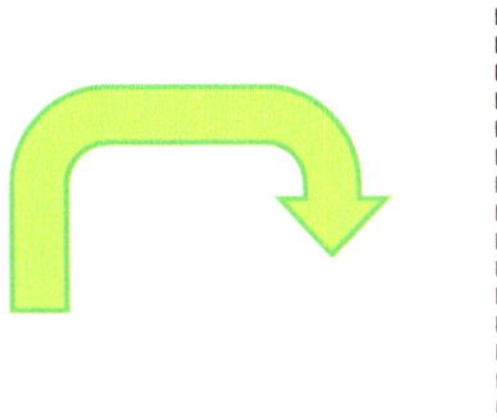

What will be its new position?

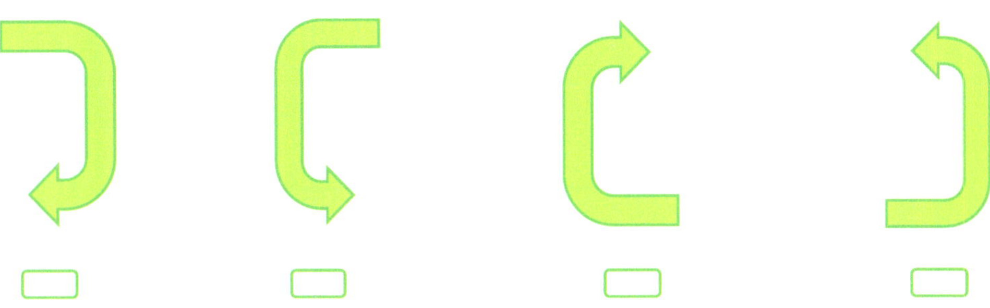

29 4 mangoes and 5 papayas cost $14. If 1 mango and 1 papaya cost $3.20, find the cost of 1 mango.

☐

30 Andrew has three different shirts, three different pants and three different shoes.

How many different combinations of shirts, pants and shoes can he choose to wear?

31 A square sheet of paper has been folded twice and the shaded area has been cut out.

If the sheet was opened, what would it look like?

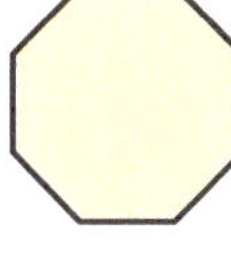

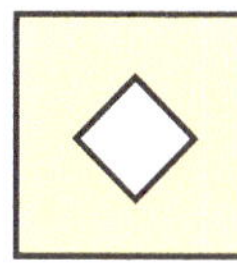

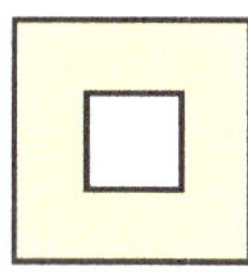

32 Steve takes vitamin tablets. He takes Vitamin C every 9 hours, Vitamin B every 8 hours and Vitamin D every 6 hours.

If he took all three at 10 pm on Sunday, when will he next take them all together?

- ☐ 10 am on Wednesday
- ☐ 10 am on Thursday
- ☐ 10 pm on Wednesday
- ☐ 10 pm on Thursday

33 Three coats are randomly given to the three people who own them. What is the probability that all of them receive their own coat?

1 in 3	1 in 6	1 in 9	1 in 12
☐	☐	☐	☐

34 Which of the following gives you the smallest number?

- ☐ 100 plus 0.1
- ☐ 100 minus 0.1
- ☐ 100 multiplied by 0.1
- ☐ 100 divided by 0.1

35 A train that is one kilometre long is travelling at 60 km/h. How long will the train take to completely pass through a tunnel that is two kilometres long?

36 How many squares of any size are there on this board?

9 ☐ 14 ☐ 18 ☐ 27 ☐

37 Two dice are thrown and the numbers added together.

What is the most likely total?

6 ☐ 7 ☐ 9 ☐ 12 ☐

38 In the diagram below the shaded part is worth 3.

What is the value of the whole rectangle?

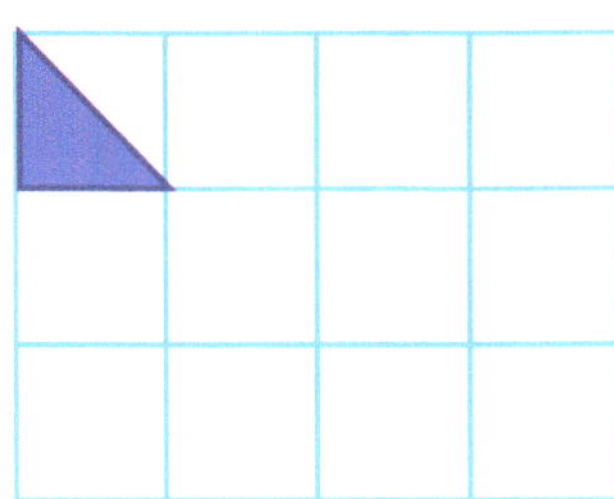

12 ☐ 36 ☐ 48 ☐ 72 ☐

39 The prices below are the full price of some items.
Amy bought the TV at a discount of 20%, the smart phone at a discount of 30% and the clock at a discount of 40%.

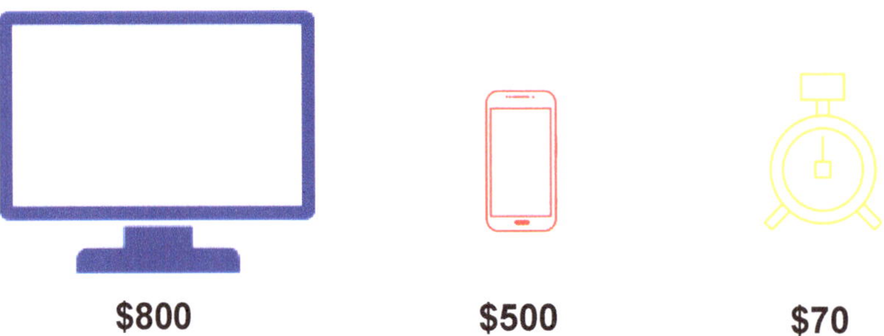

How much did she pay for the three items in total after the discount?

40 The diagram below shows two rectangles. The first rectangle is 4 cm wide and 5 cm long.

The other rectangle is 8 cm long and 2 cm wide. They are glued together to form the shaded figure shown below.

What is the area of the shaded figure?

4 cm

5 cm

2 cm

8 cm

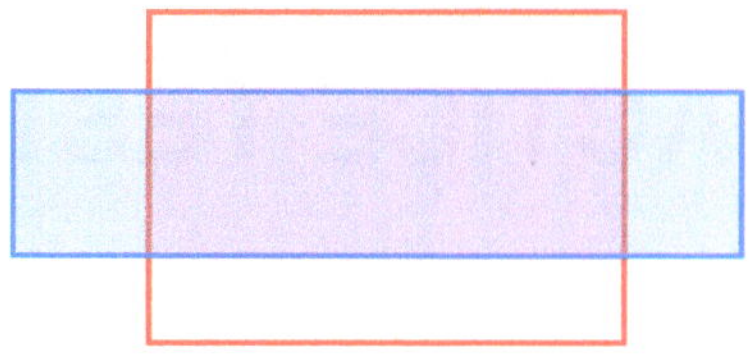

The shaded figure

☐ cm^2

NUMERACY PRACTICE TEST ANSWERS

NAPLAN Practice Test Answers
NUMERACY 1

Question	Answer	Explanation
1	C	Every letter accounts for a 0.2 increase, therefore $\frac{3}{5}$ is equivalent to 0.6 which is C.
2	1:00 pm	1 car takes 15 minutes. 10 cars take 150 minutes (2 hours 30 minutes). 2 hours and 30 minutes from 10:30 is 1:00 pm.
3	$17.30	1 orange costs 45c. 6 oranges cost $2.70. $20 – $2.70 = $17.30
4	246	1203 + 765 = 1968 buttons $\frac{1968}{8}$ = 246 buttons in each box
5	500	October = 800 cars sold August = 300 cars sold Difference = 800 – 300 = 500
6	5	25 + 58 + 17 + 45 = 145 participating members 150 – 145 = 5 nonparticipating members
7	$105	15 + (15 × 6) = $105
8	3	$\frac{75}{25} = 3$
9	(16 × 20) + (16 × 8)	
10	12:45 pm	1:30 pm – 45 minutes = 12:45 pm
11	$6	$8 \times \frac{1}{4} + 6 \times \frac{2}{3}$ = $6
12	12	4 does not go into 6. 3 does not go into 8. 4 does not go into 21.
13	$3\frac{1}{6}$ kg	$4\frac{3}{6} - 1\frac{2}{6} = 3\frac{1}{6}$
14	12.58 km	$\frac{37.74}{3}$ = 12.58 km

15	250	$200 \div 80 \times 100 = 250$
16	\$108	8 × \$13.50 = \$108
17	\$24.80 per 8 kg bag	Bag 1 = \$5/kg Bag 2 = \$4/kg Bag 3 = \$3.40/kg Bag 4 = \$3.10/kg ∴ Bag 4 (\$24.80 per 8 kg bag) is the most economical.
18	40 cm	$5 \times 8 = 40$ cm
19	60 g	5 chocolates = 300 g 1 chocolate = 60 g
20	7.5 cm^2	$(1 \times 5) + (\frac{1}{2} \times 1 \times 2) + (\frac{1}{2} \times 1 \times 3) = 7.5$ cm^2
21	10	Each number = 30° 300° = 10 hours 12 am/pm + 10 hours = 10 am/pm
22	\$12	Let x represent Chan. Sam = $2x$ Chan = x Dan = $x - 3$ Pam = $x + 17$ $(2x) + (x) + (x - 3) + (x + 17) = 74$ $5x + 14 = 74$ $5x = 60$ $x = 12$
23	66	$21 \times 3 - 8 + 2 + 9 = 66$
24	16 cm	$20 \div 5 \times 4 = 16$ cm
25	5	$(9 \times 3 - 9 + 2) \div 4 = 5$
26	4	$15 \times 16 = 240$ minutes 240 minutes = 4 hours
27	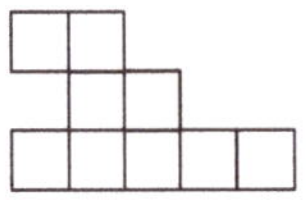 Front view	
28	512 cm^3	$8 \times 8 \times 8 = 512$ cm^3
29	8	$2^3 = 8$

30	37.5%	$25\% + \frac{25}{2}\% = 37.5\%$
31	45	$\frac{52 + 14 + 69}{3} = 45$
32	10.45°C	
33	54 centimetres	$13.5 \times 4 = 54$ cm
34	a parallelogram	
35	Chris	$(5 \times 9) - (7 \times 3) = 24$ tiles 24 tiles = Chris
36	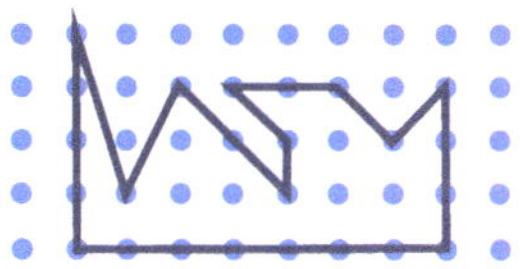	
37	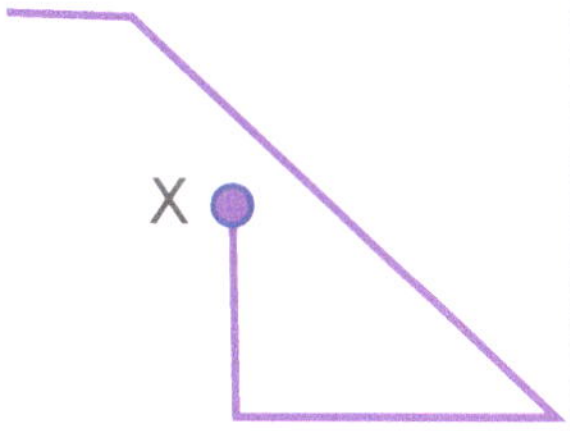 X	
38	1.2 kg	$\frac{1}{4}$ kg = 300 g 1 kg = 1200 g 1200 g = 1.2 kg
39	triangles	
40	(8, 2)	

NAPLAN Practice Test Answers
NUMERACY 2

Question	Answer	Explanation
1	15.75 m	45 cm × 35 = 1575 cm 1575 cm = 15.75 m
2	$0.25	$6.80 + $2.95 = $9.75 $10 – $9.75 = $0.25
3	8419	
4	1651 mL	5000 – 1349 = 3651 mL 3651 – 2000 = 1651 mL
5	12	7 + 5 = 12
6	$240	300 – (300 × 20%) = $240
7	Benny	Benny drinks the least amount of water for the distance ran.
8	$620	320 + (25 × 12) = $620
9	$\frac{1}{2}$	1 – 0.375 = 0.625 $\frac{0.625}{5} = \frac{1}{8}$ $\frac{3}{8} + \frac{1}{8} = \frac{4}{8} = \frac{1}{2}$
10	25	$\frac{10}{2} \times 5 = 25$
11	$23.85	$7.95 × 3 = $23.85
12	36	6 × 9 = 54 $\frac{9\times4}{2} = 18$ 54 – 18 = 36
13	4:30 pm	9:00 + 7:30 = 16:30 16:30 = 4:30 pm
14	a hexagonal pyramid	

15	5 2 5 2 5 2	
16	216	$6 \times 6 \times 6 = 216$
17		All have 6 sides.
18	16	
19	Henry	
20	ten and half turns	$7 \times 1.5 = 10.5$
21	18 minutes	The purchase must've been made between 15 and 20 minutes.
22	72	$12 \times 6 = 72$
23	33	$(5.5 + 2.75) \times 4 = 33$
24	300	$3100 - 2800 = 300$
25	Cycling	
26	It is a draw between Division 1 and 2.	Div. 1 = 98 + 265 = 363 points Div. 2 = 174 + 189 = 363 points ∴ Draw
27	Car D	Car A = 30 km/hr Car B = 30 km/hr Car C = 30 km/hr Car D = 40 km/hr ∴ Car D has the highest average speed.
28	One chance in ten	$\frac{5}{50} = \frac{1}{10}$
29	18	
30	2 hours	$\frac{1}{12} \times 24$ hours = 2 hours
31	9 and 23	$9 \times 2 + 23 \times 3 = 87$

32	70 cents	$\frac{13}{18} = 0.72... \approx 0.70$c
33	Diver 4	Diver 1 = 80 + 90 = 170 Diver 2 = 75 + 75 = 150 Diver 3 = 80 + 70 = 150 Diver 4 = 90 + 85 = 175
34	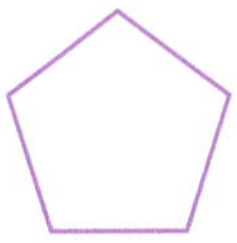	
35	33	8 am => 6 pm = 10 hours 10 g + (2.3 g × 10) = 33 g
36	0.09 is equivalent to $\frac{9}{1000}$	
37	200 g	bottle + $\frac{1}{2}$ of water = 300 g bottle + $\frac{1}{4}$ of water = 250 g $\therefore \frac{1}{4}$ of water = 50 g bottle = 250 g – 50 g = 200 g
38	2	30 – (21 + 17 – 10) = 2
39	8 cm	112 ÷ 7 ÷ 2 = 8 cm
40	Soccer	

NAPLAN Practice Test Answers
NUMERACY 3

Question	Answer	Explanation
1	12 and 24	
2	12	108 ÷ 9 = 12
3	90°	
4	$20	$180 × $\frac{40}{360}$ = $20
5	$15	$180 × $\frac{30}{360}$ = $15
6	$\frac{1}{4}$	$\frac{4}{4+5+7}=\frac{1}{4}$
7	Blue, Red, Red	Option 1 = 15 Option 2 = 13 Option 3 = 13 Option 4 = 17 ∴ Option 4
8	8	800 × 5 × 2 = 8000 m 8000 m = 8 km
9	15	(25 + 5) ÷ 2 = 15
10	45	72 – (70 – 43) = 45
11	58 cm	5 × 8 + 3 × 6 = 58 cm
12	57	57 is not divisible by 8.
13	$\frac{6}{18},\frac{6}{19},\frac{6}{20},\frac{6}{25},\frac{3}{15}$	Convert $\frac{3}{15}$ into $\frac{6}{30}$ so numerators are all 6.
14	2.5 cm	$\frac{\sqrt[3]{125}}{2}=2.5$ cm
15	13	3 × Y = 4 × 9 + 18 ÷ 6 3 × Y = 39 Y = 13
16	$\frac{5}{8}$	Convert all fractions to denominators of 8.

17	2	Only 72 and 144 are multiples of 8 and 9.
18	9	
19	168	$\frac{96}{4} \times 7 = 168$
20	15	
21	150	$6 \times 5 \times 5 = 150$
22	2.4	2.960 – 0.560 = 2.4 kg
23	$\frac{7}{18}$	$\frac{3.5}{9} = \frac{7}{18}$
24	146 to the nearest 10	Option A = 200 Option B = 149 Option C = 150 Option D = 160 ∴ Option C
25	22	130 – 45 – 35 – 28 = 22
26	Monday	
27	6	9 is not a factor of 12. 18 is not a factor of 12. 6 is a higher factor than 3.
28	10 minutes	2:50 pm => 4:45 pm = 1 hour 55 minutes 1 hour 55 minutes – 1 hour 45 minutes = 10 minutes
29	128 m^2	$4 \times 4 \times 8 = 128$ m^2
30	$1\frac{1}{12}$	$2 - \frac{3}{4} - \frac{1}{6} = \frac{13}{12}$ $\frac{13}{12} = 1\frac{1}{12}$
31	128°	180 – (90 – 38) = 128°
32	A triangular prism has two triangular faces.	
33	1 chance in 4	2 chances in 8 = 1 chance in 4
34	12	
35	8	

36	South-east	Draw a compass.
37	40 km	20 + 20 = 40
38	20 km/h	$\frac{20}{1} = 20$
39	Is it a prime number?	
40	Is it a composite number?	

NAPLAN Practice Test Answers
NUMERACY 4

Question	Answer	Explanation
1	1100	$20 \times 100 - 90 \times 10$ $= 2000 - 900$ $= 1100$
2	312	$6864 \div 22 = 312$
3	7	
4	32 cm	9 squares = 36 cm^2 1 square = 4 cm^2 Side of 1 square = 2 cm 2 x 16 = 32 cm
5	1 hour	George = 10 lollies/hr Brother = 5 lollies/hr 15 lollies = 1 hour
6	4	5, 11, 13, 29
7	Wednesday	Monday = 9°C change Tuesday = 9°C change Wednesday = 10°C change Thursday = 3°C change
8	4	6b + 8s = 50 Trial and error
9	12	
10	10	$25 - 9 - 6 = 10$
11	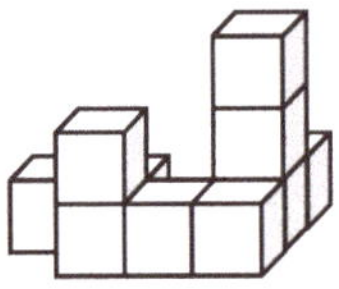	
12	24 m	The total of the horizontal sides is 12 m and the total of the vertical sides is also 12 m. ∴ Total perimeter is 24 m.

13	The original number must have ended in a 3 and a 7	Trial and error
14	594	973 – 379 = 594
15		
16		Toys in graph D make up the largest proportion compared to the other graphs.
17	\$75.00	5 kg = \$35.00 (13 – 5) kg × \$5 = \$40.00 \$35 + \$40 = \$75.00
18	\$25	150 + 6x = 300 6x = 150 x = \$25
19	3 × 8 + 6 × 10	Trial and error
20	4.2	$\frac{3.5 + 5.2 + 3.9}{3}$ = 4.2
21	3.75 m	5 × $(1 - \frac{1}{4})$ = 3.75 m
22	\$180	$\frac{45}{25}$ × 100 = \$180
23	the number divided by 75 then multiplied by 100	The number divided by 75 then multiplied by 100 = $\frac{4}{3}$
24	\$43.40	(5 × 6) + (0.5 × 18.40) + (1.4 × 3) = \$43.40
25	1.18	1.73 – 0.55 = 1.18 kg
26	1.5 kg for \$33.60	Option 1 = \$32/kg Option 2 = \$24.60/kg Option 3 = \$32.40/kg Option 4 = \$22.40/kg Therefore, option 4 is cheapest.

27	63°	360 (Sum of quadrilateral) = 117 × 2 + 2x 360 = 234 + 2x 126 = 2x x = 63°
28	144	12 × 12 = 144
29	20%	$\frac{10+20}{25+40+15+10+30+20+10} = \frac{30}{150}$ $\frac{30}{150}$ = 20%
30	10%	Cricket = $\frac{30}{150}$ Basketball = $\frac{15}{150}$ Difference = $\frac{30}{150} - \frac{15}{150} = \frac{15}{150}$ $\frac{15}{150}$ = 10%
31	(3, 2)	X axis before Y axis (horizontal before vertical)
32	28	front: 7 back: 7 top: 4 bottom: 4 right side: 3 left side: 3 ∴ 7 + 7 + 4 + 4 + 3 + 3 = 28
33	They are facing the same direction.	Dennis (Initial) = 0° or 360° (North) Andrew (Initial) = 180° (South) Dennis (After) = 0° + 90° = 90° (East) Andrew (After) = 180° − 90° = 90° (East)
34	170 cm^2	(18 × 11) – (7 × 4) = 170 cm^2
35	Octagon	New shape has 8 sides. Pentagon = 5 Hexagon = 6 Heptagon = 7 Octagon = 8
36	There is an even chance of it landing on a number greater than 3.	$> 3 = \frac{5}{8}$ $\leq 3 = \frac{3}{8}$ $\frac{5}{8} \neq \frac{3}{8}$

37	19	$1 + 3 \times (n - 1)$ Where n = Shape number
38	$5\frac{1}{2}$ or 5.5	Arrived at 10 am, left at 3:30 pm 10 am => 3:30 pm = 5 hours 30 minutes
39	4 cm	$72 \div 18 = 4$ cm
40	4th August	15 July + 20 days = 4th August

NAPLAN Practice Test Answers
NUMERACY 5

Question	Answer	Explanation
1	16	$4 \times 4 = 16$
2		Quadrilateral = 4 sides Option 1 = 5 sides Option 2 = 6 sides Option 3 = 5 sides Option 4 = 4 sides
3	72°	$\frac{360°}{5} = 72°$
4	56 cm	14 + 14 + 7 + 7 + 7 + 7 = 56 cm
5		Draw a compass rose with north facing left.
6	0.1 mm	$\frac{3}{300} = 0.01$ cm 0.01 cm = 0.1 mm
7	50	By observation, sheep make up approximately half of the graph, therefore ~ 50% 50% x 100 = 50 (Could use ruler to determine proportion)
8	$70	1st month = $10 (+10) 2nd month = $25 (+15) 3rd month = $45 (+20) 4th month = $70 (+25)
9	22 units	Number of units completed = 40 10 boxes Each box = 4 units Therefore, Days 1 and 2 = 5.5 boxes $5.5 \times 4 = 22$ units
10	$4\frac{1}{2}$ or 4.5 hours	Alan + Alex + Aiden = 12 Hours Aiden = $\frac{1}{4}$ of 12 = 3 hours Alex + Alan = 9 hours Therefore, they each painted 4.5 hours.

11	\$600	Food (%) = (100 − 50 − 25 − 5 − 5) = 15% 15% × 4000 = \$600
12	Emma	Emma = $\frac{17}{20}$ = 85% Ava = $\frac{8}{10}$ = 80% Evelyn = $\frac{12}{15}$ = 80% Flora = $\frac{4}{5}$ = 80%
13	A, B, D, C	Turn all into 24-hour time A = 06:50 B = 15:45 C = 16:30 D = 16:05
14	1332	111 + 112 + 121 + 122 + 211 + 212 + 221 + 222 = 1332
15	40 minutes	$\frac{28}{4} \times 5$ = 35 minutes 35 + 5 (himself) = 40 minutes
16	Della	Elia = 36 ÷ 3 = 12 Murphy = 48 ÷ 6 = 8 Clover = 55 ÷ 5 = 11 Della = 60 ÷ 4 = 15
17	5:15 pm	3:45 + 1:30 = 5:15 pm
18	5	200 = (5 × 0) + (1 × 10) + (2 × 40) + (3 × 30) + (4 × N) 200 = 10 + 80 + 90 + 4N 20 = 4N N = 5
19	20	Less than 2 books = 15 students More than 2 books = 35 students 35 − 15 = 20 students
20	\$6.90	(0.50 × 8) + (0.20 × 10) + (0.10 × 4) + (0.05 × 10) = \$6.90
21	33.3%	Amount of squares left = 5 Amount of shapes left = 15 $\frac{5}{15} = 33.3\%$ (Rounded to 1 d.p.)

22	6	$\frac{2}{\frac{15-7}{24}} = 6$
23		
24	6	Centre block of each face
25	7	Heart = Multiplication Star = Subtraction Circle = Addition Middle star = 25 – 18 = 7
26	30	3 + 7 + 20 = 30
27	160	$420 \times (\frac{7}{7} - \frac{3}{7}) = 240$ $240 \times (\frac{3}{3} - \frac{1}{3}) = 160$
28		
29	$2.00	Let x = Mangoes, y = Papayas $4x + 5y = 14$ $x + y = 3.20$ (Solve simultaneously) $4(3.20 - y) + 5y = 14$ $12.80 - 4y + 5y = 14$ $1.20 = y$ $x + 1.20 = 3.20$ $x = 2$
30	27	$3^3 = 27$
31		
32	10 pm on Wednesday	Let all Vitamins = Common multiple of 24 Vitamin C = 9 × 8 = 72 Vitamin B = 8 × 9 = 72 Vitamin D = 6 × 12 = 72 72 hours = 3 days 10 pm Sunday + 3 days = 10 pm Wednesday

33	1 in 6	$\frac{1}{3} \times \frac{1}{2} \times \frac{1}{1} = \frac{1}{6}$
34	100 multiplied by 0.1	Option A = 100.1 Option B = 99.9 Option C = 10 Option D = 1000
35	3 minutes	60 km/hr = 1 km/minute 2 km = 2 minutes + 1 minute (considering the end of the train passing through the tunnel)
36	14	9 (1×1), 4 (2×2), 1 (3×3) 9 + 4 + 1 = 14
37	7	Sum of 6 = (1+5), (2+4), (3+3), (4+2), (5+1) Sum of 7 = (1+6), (2+5), (3+4), (4+3), (5+2), (6+1) Sum of 9 = (3+6), (4+5), (5+4), (6+3) Sum of 12 = (6+6)
38	72	Half of 1×1 = 3 Whole of 1×1 = 6 12 1×1's = 12 × 6 = 72
39	$1032	(800 × 80%) + (500 × 70%) + (70 × 60%) = $1032
40	26	(5 × 4) + (3 × 2) = 26 (Assume that the 5 cm in the red cancels out 5 cm of the 8 cm in the blue)

Notes